THE NEW EXPORT MARKETER

THE NEW
EXPORT
MARKETER

GEORGE YOUNG

KOGAN
PAGE

First published in 1991

Kogan Page Limited
120 Pentonville Road
London N1 9JN

British Library Cataloguing in Publication Data
A CIP record for this book is available from the
British Library.

ISBN 0-7494-0380-2

Typeset by DP Photosetting, Aylesbury, Bucks
Printed and bound in Great Britain by
Martins of Berwick, Berwick upon Tweed

◀ CONTENTS ▶

◀ INTRODUCTION ▶

Strangely, the stimulus to export is most likely to come from outside a company. Perhaps an unsolicited enquiry arrives from overseas. A quotation is given. An export house is contacted. A few orders are delivered. Other orders follow spasmodically, often small in size. A member of the sales staff is sent to a local trade fair in the importing country. An advert is placed in one or two foreign journals. Eventually, the original stimulus, whatever its cause, subsides. The orders no longer arrive. The costs are written off and the affair is forgotten. The clerical staff breathe a sigh of relief: no more intractable documents and incomprehensible phone calls. Only the sales manager is left with the wistful thought that perhaps some of the older machines no longer selling could have been dumped abroad. Essentially, the firm returns to what it knows best, its all-too-familiar customer base.

The stimulus to export usually comes from outside.

The pattern described is not untypical of the first encounter of a firm with an overseas market. The failure to establish a long-term presence in that market can be traced to two flawed conceptions of what exporting is about. The first is what we might call the *passive* conception. The company believes that all it needs to do is to signal its presence overseas in an advert or two and then wait for the orders to come flooding in. It has a willing accomplice in the second conception. This we might call the *off-load* conception. It effectively ensures that any incoming orders from overseas have a long wait, until what cannot be sold on the home market is made available to the sales manager to sell abroad.

To a company used to servicing a home market, exporting is a form of innovation. Those successful in starting export drives tend to be more

Exporting is a form of innovation.

entrepreneurial than their peers, more creative, greater risk-takers, more energetic, ready at all times to keep a pulsing momentum behind the enterprise, and, above all, more cosmopolitan in vision. They are not alone in these qualities. They tend to work in an environment that is receptive to diversity and change. The environment may not be one of unalloyed success: success creates its own inertia.

Consider, for example, a company which has found a profitable niche in its home market, supplying the consistent and uniform orders of one or two large and dependable buyers. Sudden immersion overseas could well destroy its equilibrium; it might encounter a wide and often shifting range of customer demands. Unused to such complications in its business, it might fail to respond rapidly enough unless, as in Eastern Europe perhaps, the orders are of a size and uniformity to which it is accustomed.

Against this, set a smaller, less specialised, some would say less effective company, which has spent its time selling to a varied clientele with a changing product range and inevitable higher unit costs. In many ways, such a company would be better fitted to respond, at least initially, to the demands of an export enterprise.

However, no opportunistic sense of mission can be effective without good planning. To be successful, in this, as in other fields, you need to be not only a visionary but also a planner. In large firms, what passes for planning is often a cycle of committees and reports which pursue one another in a wearisome round, which really prevents rapid response to the external environment. Such a luxury is forbidden to the small company where people are a scarce resource and any export organisation is, therefore, in the beginning at least, rudimentary. In the smallest companies, with a turnover of less than £1 million per annum, the managing director can often be found handling the entire enterprise with the sole assistance of one of the clerical staff. Later, increased turnover compels some delegation of the task, usually to one of the sales staff. It is rare at this stage for anything approaching an export department to exist. In fact, if you are a small firm, it is better not to set up such a department but to make a virtue of necessity and involve as many staff as possible in the enterprise. Only in this way will your

Develop a collective sense of mission in your export enterprise.

company develop a collective sense of mission in the enterprise, which, as we have seen, is often a key to entrepreneurial success.

If you are a small firm, the pressure of exporting on your resources may seem daunting at first, but once you start to plan your export strategy you will realise to your surprise that you have distinct advantages over your larger competitors. To begin with, you will almost certainly be less heavily bureaucratised. Size and bureaucracy tend to go together. Free of the endless cycle of meetings and discussions which slow down the decision-making process in larger companies, you have the power to accelerate your response to rapid changes in the market. Operating with a smaller clientele, you will have learnt how to develop the kind of customer rapport which enables you to supply products and services to more personalised specifications. Finally, remember you are not committed to such long production runs. Economies of scale may reduce the unit costs of your bigger neighbours but they also prevent them from going for the narrow niches in the market. And it is precisely these kinds of opportunity which are likely to open up. Thus, with the right attitude and careful planning, the small firm with a marketable product has less to lose and everything to play for in the export field.

◀ CHAPTER 1 ▶

EXPORT MARKETING

Marketing strategy

A *market* is the collection of individuals who can be induced to buy a product or service. The purpose of a business operating in a market is to turn those individuals into customers for its particular product or service and then hold them in that relationship to it. The management process which pursues this objective is *marketing*. In a nutshell, it is the process which first identifies and then pursues profitable customers.

Marketing is the process which first identifies and then pursues profitable customers.

Marketing should not be confused with *selling*, which is merely the final stage which completes the process by bringing those customers to the act of purchase. To get this distinction clear in your mind, imagine trying to sell a product for which demand is in decline. No matter how hard the sell, it would not sustain demand over time. In fact, it would diminish it. Admittedly, finding a demand for your product is often a part of selling, but sustaining and developing it over time requires a *marketing strategy*.

Marketing focus

To undertake any kind of marketing strategy a market – rather than a product – focus is required. These represent two attitudes at opposite ends of a scale. At one end are companies who start by choosing the products they can sell most efficiently – that is, with maximum output from minimum input – and then rely on price, promotion, a hard sell or a cutting technical edge to get the customer to buy them. In other words,

13

they try to get the customer to want what they have to offer. At the other, marketing, end are those companies who begin where the others leave off. They start by exploring what their customers want, plan a strategy to meet those wants and then either modify their product or create a new one to meet them. Most companies, of course, fall somewhere in between these two extremes, but success in exporting involves, very definitely, a shift towards the marketing end. If you want success in this field, you will need to examine your operation closely to see just where it lies along the continuum and then decide how you can shift it just that bit further towards the marketing end.

Success in exporting involves a market rather than a product focus.

Inevitably, there is a trade-off between marketing viewed in this light and production and finance. In your production to date, you may have tried to increase your operating efficiency by ensuring as little variation as possible in the production process. To put it simply, you will have gone for economies of scale. In itself there is nothing wrong with this as an operating principle, but it clearly runs counter to marketing strategy, which has as its sales objective a maximum of choice in the product line to satisfy customer needs.

With finance, too, there are points of conflict. In the past, you will at times no doubt have tried to reduce your stocks to a minimum to save on working capital. This is another worthy motive which all the textbooks will applaud, but it has the unfortunate effect of often limiting the availability of the product range to potential customer needs. It is a worrying thought that a recent survey found so many accountants in charge of UK companies. One shudders at the thought of what their cost accounting may be doing to marketing strategy.

Marketing effectiveness

Essentially, each of these trade-offs reveals a fundamental conflict between *productive efficiency*, measured in terms of maximum output from minimum input, and *marketing effectiveness*, which can only be gauged in the final analysis by how successful you are in creating and keeping customers. In a stable market environment, the conflict is rarely apparent, but in the modern world, markets have a limited life expectancy. Consequently, when markets change, ineffective companies are destined to die. The process may be slowed by increasing efficiency through cut-backs and retrenchment but the ultimate outcome is only delayed.

Marketing effectiveness is gauged by how successful you are in creating and keeping customers.

A less efficient but more effective company will have a better chance of survival in a new environment. It is just such an environment which confronts the first-time exporter, which is why a highly efficient adaptation to a home market base is no guarantee of success in the venture. The cultural and geographical distance of potential customers demands an orientation less to efficiency and more to marketing effectiveness; a sensitivity, in fact, an ability to read and then learn from the faintest signals of customer need.

International marketing

The same product–market scale also distinguishes between export marketing and international marketing, which lies still further towards the pole of marketing effectiveness.

The export marketer seeks to increase the sale of his company's products abroad to maximise volume and thereby reduce his overall unit costs. The aim is usually to sell abroad a product which has already gained market acceptance at home. Modification of the product or the previously successful marketing process is forced upon the exporter.

The international marketer, in contrast, treats the world as one large market consisting of innumerable segments and, from the beginning, develops a marketing plan to meet the needs of those segments.

An effective exporter is responsive to the needs of the international market; an effective international marketer anticipates those needs. In a global market, this must remain your ultimate ambition.

Planning a marketing strategy

The product cycle spiral
Whether marketing for the home, export or world market, you will need to *select* and *prioritise* your target markets on the basis of the customers you are planning to reach and how you are going to reach them profitably in competition with existing products.

If you are a small firm on a shoe-string budget, planning at this stage will involve you in a lot of often quite tedious market research. Once this stage is complete, you can move into those phases that lead out to the real world. You can use your data to:

- modify your product or develop a new one;
- price it;
- promote it;

15

- distribute it;
- plan any after-sales service.

The four Ps of your marketing strategy should be: product, price, promotion, place.

These stages have been popularised as the four Ps of:

- product
- price
- promotion
- place or distribution.

(Sometimes an S is included for service.) Each of the four Ps will engage you in a cluster of activities which work towards the general objective for that stage of the operation.

Take distribution, for example. This includes all those activities involved in actually getting your goods to your customers; that is, the passage of those goods through the trade structure of a new and alien market. But there is much more to it than that. Getting those goods physically to that market is going to involve you in a host of further organisational activities; in fact, the whole field of export administration, which includes:

- order-handling
- packing
- quotation
- documentation
- shipment
- finance
- insurance.

Taking each cluster in turn for each of the four Ps, you will need to decide which you can handle in parallel and which you are more or less compelled to do in some form of sequence.

Take promotional activities as an example. You can easily book advertising space while still working on your advertising copy, but you shouldn't really book this space until you have done a thorough research of all the relevant media.

Whatever you do in one area will inevitably affect outcomes in others.

The way the stages are set out does indeed suggest a natural sequence, but decision-making is never simple. Whatever you do in one area inevitably affects outcomes in others. If you fail to get perishable goods to the market in time, for example, you may be forced to dump them elsewhere at a discount. Some lucky middleman may pick up your goods there and, without your distribution problems, flood them back to their original destination at a different price. In other words, a failure of distribution is going to pull apart your pricing policy.

Each set of activities is, therefore, best thought of as connected in a chain, which causes each to impact on all the others. In marketing jargon this notion is called the *product cycle spiral*, an all-encompassing cyclical loop which returns the marketer endlessly back to a close examination of the success or otherwise of each preceding stage of the marketing exercise. Whatever the internal sequence of these activities within your organisation, their ultimate impact on the market will represent a combination of outcomes in all of them.

This combination of activities is called the *marketing mix*. The objective of marketing strategy is to present a decision 'mix' which your target customers will prefer to that of your competitors. In export marketing, of course, the problems of getting the right mix are intensified by the physical and cultural distances from the customer.

The objective of your marketing strategy is to present a decision mix which your target customers will prefer to that of your competitors.

Marketing plan

To achieve the right mix, you need to devise a *marketing plan*. Planning varies in 'range'. It may be short term, a skimming off of profits, or long term; the latter is designed to gain a more permanent share of the market. Earlier in your operation, you may have survived from day to day without giving much thought to long-term goals. A surprising number of companies pursue this pattern of life, particularly in protected niches of the home market. Indeed, it can be combined, and often is, with short-term engagement with an overseas market. However, this attitude will never serve to secure a permanent base in the export field, and it will also fail to protect the market at home one day. Export marketing can help to prepare you for the coming of that day by offering you the stimulus to develop *long-term marketing plans*.

To achieve the right mix, you need to devise a marketing plan.

Product life cycle and profitability

To be effective, any marketing strategy requires overall goals. It is not enough to seek profits. Profits are only significant once full investment recovery has taken place. How close you will ever get to recovering your investment will depend on exactly what point you entered the life cycle of the product you are selling.

All products, it has been suggested, have a life cycle of growth and subsequent decline. In the early stages, when a new product comes on the market, sales begin to take off once the first adventurous buyers start to set a pattern for a gathering number of potential customers. At this

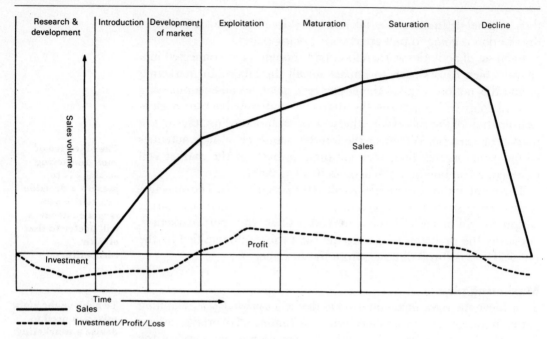

Figure 1.1 *Product life cycle*

stage of sales expansion, profit margins are often high as the lead company uses price to skim the market and rapidly recoup its outlay before competitors begin to copy their way into the field.

The entry of others may be delayed by the barriers of patents or simply by the problems of adapting to the new technology, but come they usually do and the effects are almost instantaneous. An initial boost as new variants of the product stimulate consumption is soon followed by falling profit margins as product after product enters the fight for market share. It is not long before the rate of sales expansion begins to taper. The market moves to saturation.

At the point of saturation, the shake-out begins. The life cycle of the product is entering its most turbulent phase. This is the day, you might say, of the shortest shadow. The heat is on. Some companies merge to hold their diminishing market share; others pull out of the field. As the battle cools, the market enters its mature phase. A smaller, more stable number of combatants survive but without the profits of 'the good old days'. From maturity, the cycle curves downwards, into a pattern of decline.

All products seem to pursue this cycle although time-scales differ. The breakfast cereal market has been in maturity for 20 years; the television games market is already well into its decline. As a pattern, cycles are shortening; the decline sets in faster.

When a product begins to come to the end of its life cycle before full recovery has been achieved, the company faces a serious failure. If a cycle is shortening, it is important to recover investment as rapidly as possible. In this area, exporting often serves to counterbalance a contracting home market. But it is not sufficient merely to seek sales. We have already seen how exporting tends to push you towards a focus on the market rather than the product. Similarly, long-term planning pushes you towards the marketing side of yet another conflict, this time between a marketing and a sales orientation.

Sales orientation focuses on:

- sales volume rather than profit planning;
- short-term rather than long-term gains;
- customer accounts rather than market segments;
- field-work rather than desk work.

In market orientation, these priorities are reversed, and in the export field the reversal is essential to guarantee long-term penetration of the market.

Whatever form your pursuit of profitability takes, it will be the linch-pin of your strategic framework. Without such a framework it will be impossible to create an effective export marketing mix. Instead, you will find yourself overwhelmed by a chaotic schedule of activities, all of which require the same level of urgency. Your cyclical loop will turn into an unending chain of competing demands which slowly throttles your organisational life. At the very least, a framework with clear goals will enable you to:

- specify more clearly the objectives of each element of the mix;
- develop more detailed targets, such as monthly sales targets or advertising campaign targets, which are designed to achieve them;
- create a mechanism to monitor your goals, objectives and targets;
- set a time-scale for each;
- begin the whole exercise with an analysis of your resources.

Let us begin with the analysis of resources.

◀ CHAPTER 2 ▶

PLANNING RESOURCES

Exporting is an activity which will place new demands on the resources of your company. Therefore, at the beginning of your strategic planning you need to know what you can bring to play in the markets abroad in terms of:

- production
- finance
- personnel.

Let us examine each in turn.

Production

A successful export drive will bring new orders. An important question, therefore, is:

Your company must have the capacity to fulfil orders.

- Does your company have the capacity to fulfil those orders?

If it doesn't, you may find yourself in the following situation. An Asian textile company for which I once offered myself as agent in opening up an Eastern European market suddenly found itself short of labour to man the machines and had to pull out of the operation at the eleventh hour.

Long periods of production for a stable home market have an element of inertia which ensures a steady flow of orders from familiar customers. In the export market, the customers are at first an unknown quantity. A long lull can be followed by a sudden inundation of orders, stretching your production to the limit.

- Do you have the spare capacity or the option to expand to take the pressure?
- Does your product require much servicing?

As one experienced commentator has remarked, an ideal export product should need no service. But, if some service is required:

- Do you have the resources to provide after-sales service?

Providing after-sales service overseas is never easy but it is essential if, for example, you are entering the affluent and sophisticated Northern European markets for consumer durables.

When considering an export enterprise, it is better not to make a move at all than to do so without satisfactory answers to these questions.

Finance

Many new exporters are tempted to make only a small, initial investment, but the cost of a small operation is high. A larger operation with fixed costs, overheads and management time spread over a longer projected turnover might turn out cheaper in the long run. Laying in extra raw materials and packing, covering insurance and freight charges, and delays in payment from overseas can all put extra strains on your cash flow.

- Do you have the necessary bridging finance?
- Can you support investment in initial research and travelling, the costs of which may not be recouped from the first export orders?
- Could you take an initial loss on the export side?

These are questions you need to confront in the early stages. My own experience provides a cautionary tale.

I once organised an export drive with my own company as the agent for a small consortium of computer software companies who were anxious to break into the Czech and Hungarian markets. The plan was bold in conception. My role was to open the doors by making the first contact with the planned economies, with the companies themselves following close behind with technical support. The venture, however, was undercapitalised. Failure to secure the necessary overdraft facilities caused one company to withdraw. Panic set in and the operation fell apart. All this could have been avoided if the question of finance had been confronted with brutal honesty from the start.

Finance is critical.   Exporting is a risk. Finance is critical. You need to explore all avenues from the start.

> - Are you, for instance, aware of the possibilities of export credit insurance?
> - Are you aware of the longer periods of credit generally available for export customers?
> - Do you know that some banks have developed special export finance packages?
> - Have you thought of the problems of invoicing overseas customers in other currencies and how to protect yourself against exchange rate fluctuations?

For all such issues, banks are a useful source of help and advice.

Personnel

Finally, you need to ask yourself serious questions about your personnel. The key to successful exporting is ensuring a near-constant involvement of senior management in making and keeping contact with representatives and customers. Initially, the managing director may handle the operation himself, but inevitably the development of the enterprise will involve more staff.

> - Is your firm able to cope with the absence of individuals abroad for long periods?
> - Do staff have a sufficiently international outlook?
> - Do staff have any knowledge of world markets?
> - What knowledge do they have of other languages and cultures?

Language and cultural barriers can prove insurmountable. A telephonist for a medium-sized company recently told me that in the absence of anyone able to speak a foreign language when phoning abroad, they simply held the line until someone could be brought to the other end of the line with some knowledge of English. One wonders what happened when nobody could be found.

Language is only part of the problem. If you have never exported before, your administrative staff may know little or nothing about exporting. Your local Chamber of Commerce will almost certainly run short courses on export documentation. You could hand over the administration to outside agencies, but the costs incurred will need to be built into your future projections. Generally, as we have seen, the more staff you involve in the enterprise the better, as in so doing you begin to develop an export business culture. It is such company-wide involvement which accounts for much of the success of the Japanese. Do not forget, also, that the personal touch of individual staff involved with overseas accounts is often an important factor in motivating agents and creating customer loyalty.

Concluding remarks

A close examination of these questions is essential before you commit a penny of your resources to an export enterprise. Remember that most first ventures fail because they fail to cover unforeseen costs, not because they do not reach their originally projected levels of profit. In other words, they fail because they are underresourced, underpowered if you like, for the enterprise in hand. A worthwhile examination requires a certain brutal honesty. There is an old saying among gardeners: 'Let your worst enemy prune your roses.'

Extend this image to the business world. Let your worst enemy prune your fantasies. If you have not got an enemy, an accountant or bank manager will do. Talk the whole scheme over with someone whose ego is not involved in the operation; someone who will give you a purely actuarial perspective. In fact, talk to as many people as possible while the thought is still budding in your mind.

Your area may have a local exporters club. If so, join it. If you have not done so already, join your local Chamber of Commerce. More business is done at its dinners than anywhere else in some provincial cities. Talk with experienced exporters. Open your mind to them but always listen, listen and take note. That way, you will learn from others' mistakes.

Convinced of the strength of your case and with a cautiously optimistic eye to the future, you can begin the first stage of the export enterprise.

◀ CHAPTER 3 ▶

MARKET RESEARCH

Knowledge is power. In marketing, it is the power to plan and execute a marketing strategy. Where that strategy fails, it is often because the marketing mix has been based on inadequate knowledge of the market environment. The market environment includes all factors in a territory which affect firms competing within it. Information can be gathered from a number of sources using desk research first and then personal reconnaissance.

Desk research

You can, if you wish, commission research from a marketing consultancy, but remember that research offers no direct contribution to revenue. Furthermore, most of the information you require has already been published and is accessible at little cost from government agencies and other export-oriented bodies, or even from your local library. As an operating principle, try to spend as much time but as little money as you can, and begin your searches with the cheapest and most easily accessible sources.

Research offers no direct contribution to revenue.

All rational desk research involves the construction and administration of a database. A large company may be able to afford to set up an export research department. Such a step not only involves heavy costs without a direct contribution to revenue but also tends to hive off the export drive as a specialised interest of a few staff. To create greater involvement, rather than set up such a unit in a small company, it is better to delegate aspects of the research task to particular individuals.

Get the sales staff, for example, to collect information on customers, and the clerical staff to gather information on export documentation. To prevent duplication of effort, have a central database where the results are filed under the control of at least one member of staff who has a watching brief over the entire research enterprise.

Personal reconnaissance

There is no substitute for on-the-spot data collection.

Ultimately, there is no substitute for on-the-spot data collection. This is particularly so for capital goods exporters who really need to discuss specific customer requirements on the spot. Living and working in a country is obviously the best guarantee of in-depth knowledge of its market environment, which is why very few people can truthfully claim up-to-date knowledge of more than one or two markets.

Market sector features can change very rapidly. Take this country as an example. Where was the 'environmental' dimension in marketing a decade ago? Where was the 'European' dimension a decade before that? The only way that a small company without permanent connections abroad can pick up on such developments is to make a carefully planned visit to reconnoitre the market. There is an old saying that good intelligence is never wasted in war. To prevent wastage, however, good planning is essential. But first you must think about the following.

Clarify the objectives of the visit

This saves time and money. Too often, first-time exporters send someone out on an escapade which is something between market research and an exercise in personal recreation. Anyone sent abroad needs a set of clear directives of places to visit, things to see and, even more importantly, people to meet, with a checklist of questions to be answered in each case.

Know the best time to visit

Public holidays may vary across the world but they always have the same impact. Can you imagine a foreign business man on a visit to a Lancashire mill town during the July holiday fortnight? Mediterranean saints' festivals can have an equally devastating effect on local business. An exporter I know arrived in the Spanish town of Alcoy during the feast of San Jorge to find that his commercial contacts were either celebrants in the interminable succession of processions or in the local bars in varying stages of inebriation. Your visit is much better planned to occur when local business activity is particularly buoyant. Can it, for example, be made to coincide with a local trade fair? A fair may enable you to meet potential wholesalers, agents and distributors to assess competition.

Think about 'how' to visit

Think seriously about joining a trade mission. There is a constant stream of outward missions from local Chambers of Commerce to overseas markets. A local chamber mission does not simply draw on its own members or even on the locality. A Birmingham mission, for example, will often have participants from all over the country. Between a dozen and twenty or so individuals form an average mission. However, organisers often have a problem getting enough people, especially for more peripheral market destinations, and so tend to welcome any enquiries from would-be exporters.

Missions usually last about a week, but can be longer if more than one country, say, Hungary and Czechoslovakia, is visited. Travel and accommodation are included in the overall cost, which is often reduced by a government subsidy. Efforts are made to arrange contacts before-hand and the Central Office of Information (COI) is often brought in to help with publicity.

Much of the success of missions depends on the drive and energy of individual organisers but, even so, the shortfall in numbers participating is often surprising, especially for visits to Europe. Some of the best attended are the London Chamber's missions. With a good attendance, you can be sure of finding at least one other experienced fellow-traveller who could give you some good tips on the local market.

Mission involvement gains much from prior research and planning. For the new exporter, missions are an excellent way of reconnoitring the market and making some useful contacts in the process.

◀ CHAPTER 4 ▶

BUILDING THE DATABASE

A database is essential to the task of targeting and prioritising the target markets. Built up by desk research or personal reconnaissance, it should consist only of information relevant to the export drive. Figuring among this information should be:

- demographic features
- the nature of the market
- distribution channels
- retail culture
- tariff and non-tariff barriers to market entry
- market profile.

Demographic features affect the size and life cycle of market segments.

Demographic features

These affect the size and life cycle of market segments. Among the most important of them are:

Wealth
About half of the gross national product of the European Community lies in the Golden Triangle between Brest, Copenhagen and Strasbourg, which is an important fact to bear in mind if you are selling to the mass consumer market.

Life-style
How is this wealth spent? Take soap as an example. Statistically, the

Greeks have been found to use less than the French, and the French less than the Dutch. A trivial statistic? Not if you are a company planning to sell bathroom accessories to Europe.

Urbanisation

Does your product require any after-sales service? This will be considerably easier to provide in a small, urbanised, densely populated country like Belgium than in a less urbanised, more thinly populated country like Spain.

Age structure

West Germany's population is ageing faster than that of Greece, a fact that should never be far from the mind of, for example, a manufacturer of toys for the continent.

Education

Outside Europe, levels of literacy can be very low. Consider some of the consequences. One at least is clear. You may need visual rather than verbal advertising for mass consumer goods. This does not only apply to developing countries. North American advertisers now produce copy for an assumed general standard of literacy no higher than that of a nine-year-old. If your product is in any way volatile or dangerous, it is particularly important that instructions for its use are carefully and very simply explained.

Technology

When selling to underdeveloped countries in particular, you need to ask yourself whether the market is technically advanced enough for your product. Have you thought of selling your automatic cash dispensers to a central African country? Think again. You may be surprised to find that most of the retail trade is on the streets.

The nature of the market

You need to investigate the nature, size and trend of the market, and how it is distributed among your potential competitors, looking in turn at:

You need to investigate the nature, size and trend of the market.

29

Competing products

- What is the range and width of competing product lines?
- How are competing products packaged and presented?
- What are the major selling points of competitors?
- Can you spot any limitations in the quality and finish of existing products?
- Has there been much innovation in the market-place in recent years? If not, does this point to an element of inertia in patterns of consumption?
- Have preferences frozen into loyalties?

Local loyalty to existing operators entrenches their competitive position, making them hard to dislodge. Loyalty varies across products and frontiers. Surveys reveal, for example, that the Germans are more chauvinistic buyers of cars than the French, and the French more than the Spaniards and British. You need to ask yourself what the selling points of your competitors are:

- How do they compare with yours?
- Have you a competitive edge in cost benefit or quality and service?

Price range

- What range of prices are customers prepared to pay?
- How has the price of competing products changed in the past?
- How far is it likely to move in the future?
- Could you achieve profitability within this range?

Market size

This is another indicator of potential profitability. From government production and customs statistics, and company and stockbroker reports, you can assess the domestic production capacity in your product line which, with existing import penetration minus exports, will give you a rough idea of the present ceiling to the market for your product. The ratio of imports to exports will give you an idea of how far market capacity, in terms of volume, is met by local suppliers. If you find high levels of export from the market, this could be a sign of saturation. From annual changes in sales volumes and movements in prices, you can also estimate the state of the product life cycle.

Product life cycle

We have already seen how the life of a product has serious implications for profit margins. By carefully comparing different markets for the same product, you will soon see which still have clear growth trends and which have already entered a stage of serious decline.

The picture is not quite as chaotic as it sounds. Life cycles for products do vary with their different markets, but the growth of trade and communication is tending to close the gap between them, especially within trading blocs like the Western European. Increasingly, it seems, life cycles are beginning to follow a global pattern.

All the same, you need to time your entry into your new market with the greatest care. You must ask yourself whether the phase of greatest growth is already over. If so, competitors could be entrenched and therefore able to make you pay dearly for the costs of market entry. New entrants rarely achieve high levels of profitability in established markets.

- Is there further evidence of pressures on profitability in the form of mergers and take-overs?
- Is a shake-out threatened? If so, would it be wise to enter now?

Market share

- How is the market distributed between competitors?
- What share would you need to achieve profitability in cost and price?
- Are there any segments uncatered for by existing suppliers?
- Could any such segments provide you with a profitable niche? If so, why has no one moved in before you?
- Is there something you do not know?

Distribution channels

You must know not only who your customers are but also how to reach them. Your database should contain information on:

You must know who your customers are and how to reach them.

Trade channel structures

Different countries have different channels of distribution which vary according to the type of goods sold. In some, the distribution channels are dominated by a few multiple retailers; in others, they are more dispersed. In some, the functions of wholesaling and retailing are merged with that of importing; in others, they are kept entirely distinct.

The outlets for products also vary between different countries. In some, liquor or even drugs may be sold in general stores. In others, a tobacconist may take over some of the functions of a post office or even a chemist. An exporter of speciality foods may find there is simply no local concept of a delicatessen. The products could even end up on the stalls of street vendors.

Not only do channels differ in type and mutual relations, they also vary considerably in complexity. Japan, for example, has one of the most complex distribution systems in the world. As an exporter to Japan, you may have to sell to a general wholesaler who in turn sells to a basic product speciality wholesaler; he then sells to a speciality wholesaler, from whom the goods pass to a regional wholesaler and then on to a local wholesaler, before finally ending up with the retailer. Such an extended distribution chain inevitably distances you from the ultimate consumer of your product. This is something that you may not have encountered before. You will need to take it into account in your marketing strategy.

The infrastructure of road, rail and air links

Many manufacturers choose to deliver their own goods to the overseas market. You may have already found the cheapest way of getting your goods from A to B at home, but do you know what alternatives exist overseas and how they compare in cost? Your product may have to travel over much longer distances. Would your present mode of transport necessarily suit it best? You may never have used roll-on/roll-off links and containers before. Can you find good container connections en route? Are you planning to send your own trucks abroad? Look at the road system. Think of the quality of the roads and what it means for you in time and running costs. The equivalent of German autobahns is nowhere to be found in Portugal or the Balkans.

Retail culture

Once your product arrives at its destination what will be its fate? If it passes through a retail outlet, how is it likely to be presented? Even in these days of the global market there are important cultural differences in packaging and presentation.

Research consumer preferences in presentation and packaging.

Presentation

Different countries have different *shelfing codes* in the mass consumer field. Only a visit to a few local supermarkets or retail outlets will tell you where your product is likely to end up. Have you thought that your coffee filter paper may end up somewhere between the garlic sausage and the cheese? If it does, you might decide to put new colours in your packaging. If you do, remember that the same colours and colour shades carry a different emotional significance in different cultures. The Mexicans prefer a brighter shade than the Dutch.

There are also trends in colour. Take, for example, the recent popularity of different shades of green in European advertising. Large trade fairs, like the ones at Frankfurt, can give you a good idea of the latest colour trends in such commodities as furniture and kitchen-ware.

Packaging

Colours are not only culture coded in presentation but in almost every aspect of packaging. Witness, for example, the enormous differences between North America and Europe in the packaging of a range of items from sugar to cigarettes. As a general rule, where there are preferences in packaging, it is tactically advisable to observe them. If your potential customers are used to buying their razor-blades in packs of ten, then provide them in this form.

The history of exporting is littered with disasters which followed from the failure of companies to observe or research consumer preferences in packaging and presentation. A perfect example is Kentucky Fried Chicken's first ventures into the Hong Kong market. This enterprise failed because the Chinese simply found it too alien at first to eat hot chicken with their fingers from a cardboard carton.

Generally, the richer the country the more extensive the packaging. Even holding wealth constant, there are variations in modes of presentation in the same market sectors of different countries. If you doubt this, visit an Italian motorway service station and compare its glossy and stylish shop and cafeteria precinct with its British counterpart.

Tariff and non-tariff barriers to market entry

Types of barrier

Bear in mind any barriers to market entry.

Getting your goods to the market is not just a matter of transport and distribution. You must also bear in mind any barriers to market entry; this is the point at which the dreaded word 'tariff' must be considered. You will meet two types of tariff on your travels: *specific*, which is raised on a specific unit of the goods imported; and *ad valorem*, which is calculated as a percentage of the value of a product.

Since the Kennedy round of the 1960s, tariffs have come down in many market sectors of the world; however, even where there are no tariff barriers, the market may still be highly protected. Among the richer markets, the South Koreans and the Japanese are notorious. Almost any aspect of business or technical legislation can be used by such countries to restrict market entry. Among the poorer countries, many resort to control by:

Currency restrictions and price controls

The sheer speed and unexpectedness of policy changes in currency and price control has taken many an exporter unawares and wiped away the margins of what might have been a profitable export drive.

Quotas

These are also often imposed to regulate the import of products from specific countries. Another kind of quota system operates when a government insists that a minimum percentage of local components or materials must be used in goods manufactured locally. More sinister are cartels of local distributors which exclude imported goods or 'fix' them at inflated prices.

Import permits

These are often introduced by governments to protect nascent or declining industries under pressure from local lobbies.

Health and safety standards

These can operate as a barrier to imports, often with government connivance. European harmonisation in this field still leaves much of the world unstandardised and sudden changes can create a minefield for the unsuspecting exporter, as can changes in design and materials specification.

Design and materials specifications
Horror stories abound of companies having to dismantle entire export production lines after discovering that materials or a particular design employed are prohibited by legislation in the target market.

Packaging and labelling regulations
These vary considerably across the world and are an irritating constraint on companies setting up a multi-market export drive. Such is the complexity of this problem that, even within Europe, the process of harmonisation is still incomplete. At the moment, there is a constant flow of standards legislation in the pipeline, much of which will open up new avenues in the European market.

Procurement bias
Even where there is no apparent overt pressure to appoint local contractors to public projects, tradition and the power of the electorate often lead governments to prefer to do business with their own companies. In recent years, a world lobby of opinion has built up against this kind of discrimination, leading to more transparent procedures in Europe and the first signs of outside penetration of previously heavily protected public sectors like that of Japan. Opening up the market will, of course, fail to create full equality of opportunity where local companies receive hidden subsidies to make them price competitive.

The abolition of non-tariff barriers: the European Community

The most widespread and radical abolition of non-tariff barriers occurring anywhere in the world at the moment is now in progress in the European Community (EC). Essentially, it is an exercise in deregulation by member governments and reregulation by the EC. It will involve legislation which the would-be exporter to Europe ignores at great risk. January 1993 is the target date, but the process may not be completed until the mid-1990s.

The mechanism to carry through the proposals was established by the 1987 Single European Act as one of qualified majority voting, which means that no two countries can halt proposals agreed by the others. This replaces the previous requirement for a unanimous vote on measures which have as their object the establishment and functioning of the internal market, or cover such issues as recognition of professional qualifications, free movement of capital and services, and progress in establishing a common transport policy. Unanimity is still required for decisions on the free movement of people, and the setting of excise duties and VAT rates, areas in which, as a consequence, progress towards the single market concept is likely to be slow.

The original 1985 proposals were both detailed, covering such issues as the eradication of African swine-fever in Portugal, and wide ranging, suggesting, for example, a uniform level of duty on alcohol across the EC. They fell into three main areas, concerning physical, technical and fiscal barriers to trade.

Physical barriers

The physical barriers are those of customs, police and immigration controls. Barriers such as these at internal frontiers will be removed or much reduced, although governments reserve the right to re-introduce them without notice at times of crisis – for example, during a wave of terrorist attacks. Documentation at frontier posts has already been simplified through the Single Administrative Document, which replaces about 100 forms previously used in Community trade.

Technical barriers

The technical barriers are the varying national standards which have obstructed the use of goods, the provision of services and the employment of individuals. A good example of such a barrier is the German law, the Rheinheitsgebot, which dates back to 1516. It forbids the use in beer of anything other than the traditional ingredients of barley, water, malt, hops and yeast, thereby allowing the German brewers to restrict the import of foreign beers but enabling them to export beer with chemical additives to other countries.

On 7 May 1985, the Council of Ministers adopted a resolution setting out a general operating principle to harmonise differing technical standards. This involved replacing the morass of conflicting national standards with minimum general requirements which must be satisfied before a product is sold. General standards are usually prepared by the European standards bodies CEN (European Committee for Standardisation) and CENELEC (European Committee for Electro-technical Standardisation) on the basis of 'mandates' agreed with the European Commission.

In alignment with this process, agreement was reached on a directive in 1988 to harmonise the national trade mark laws of the member states; in particular the rights conferred by registration and the grounds on which registration may be refused. Registration will be validated by an

EC trade mark system which will be registrable for the whole Community by a single procedure at the new EC trade marks office.

With differing national standards, which affect production, will also go the kinds of restriction which have always operated to stem the carriage of goods and services across frontiers. In the past, systems of quotas and permits on road haulage have led to the spectacle of empty lorries going back and forth across Europe because they are prevented from picking up return loads. In the Single European Market, hauliers will be allowed to pick up a load in any member state and deliver it to another in a condition of free and fair competition.

Freedom of movement of labour was theoretically a freedom enshrined in the Treaty of Rome but it was hindered from the beginning by the incompatibility of different standards of qualification and training. In this area, the EC has sought for compatibility rather than uniformity on the basis of mutually agreed minimum standards of training and job description for selected occupations. In the Single European Market, members of a whole range of professions, from dentists to physiotherapists, will need to qualify only once to practise throughout the EC. Similarly, new rights of establishment will enable any citizen to start a business in any member state.

Not only individual but also institutional purveyors of services will benefit from a freer flow. Progress has already been made towards a freer market in non-life insurance. A recent directive could pave the way for people to buy car insurance from other member states.

There should also be greater freedom of competitive tender for public contracts. Bias has been rife in public procurement with national governments handing multi-billion contracts for telecommunications, construction and military hardware to carefully protected national suppliers. In the future, governments will have to demonstrate fair competition in public purchasing through more transparent procedures. A number of test cases is bound to ensue.

The free movement of goods and services needs to be supported in turn by the free movement of capital, and an open market in banking and securities. In some cases, the EC is pushing an already open door. West Germany and Britain have long since abolished exchange controls. The rest of the richer member states have agreed to lift all controls on their capital movements by the mid-1990s.

Fiscal barriers
Finally, fiscal barriers to trade are probably among the most intractable.

The harmonisation of fiscal regimes will involve confronting the difficult problems of excise duties and different levels of indirect taxation. A number of proposals have already been made for dealing with VAT. The most interesting to date suggests a harmonisation of VAT rates within broad tax bands. Even more divergent than VAT, excise duties will also need to be progressively harmonised.

The new Europe

- What kind of Europe will confront the UK exporter once all this legislative activity has run its course?
- What kind of European economy will have emerged by then?
- To what kind of world will the UK supplier have to adapt in order to survive?
- What new potential will there be to exploit?
- What new problems will there be to confront?

To begin with, it will be a world offering the possibility of much greater rationalisation in production for the overseas market. In the past, different standards of safety and pollution have required modifications in production to meet them. A good example is the Volvo plant in Ghent, Belgium, making trucks for Europe. To satisfy the different standards, it has had to make eight basic models with 84 versions and 235 separate certificates. Harmonisation of standards should mean fewer product lines and, of course, fewer labelling and packaging designs.

Rationalisation should produce economies of scale which will also be enlarged by the wider market-oriented companies driving out the smaller and often less efficient companies who have hitherto been protected by trade barriers. At the moment, such barriers to fair competition have allowed over 50 European tractor manufacturers in different national segments to fight over a market bigger than that of the United States, in which competition has reduced the number of contenders to no more than four. It has been the same story in the field of domestic appliances. In Europe, there are over 300 main suppliers; in the United States, once again, there are only four.

Products will also get to their destination more quickly. The already weakening barriers on shipping and road haulage should see to that.

Money, too, should flow more freely. Ordering and invoicing will probably be computerised.

Loosening restrictions on data exchange networks such as electronic banking systems will allow greater freedom to use the public telephone networks to exchange information.

Competition should also bring down prices. Why is the price of West German telecommunication equipment so far above world market levels? All such anomalies should be less in evidence in the Europe of the nineties. If prices fall, and both competition and the free flow of capital truly act as catalysts to growth, then the dream of national governments may occur in the form of an extended run of non-inflationary expansion.

It is difficult to say how large the projected growth will be. Projections by economists committed to the ideal of a Single European Market are optimistically based on a series of multiplier effects operating like a chain reaction. The best-case contingency forecast puts the gain from the freedom to buy in the cheapest and sell in the dearest market at around two to three percentage points of the EC gross domestic product (GDP), a gain which is then doubled by the addition of two broader effects: economies of scale and the reduction of overmanning and inefficiency caused by protective barriers. If governments take advantage of the release of these extra productive resources to adopt more expansionary policies, the GDP could increase by seven percentage points without any risk of inflation or deterioration in public finance. In other words, a chain reaction sets in, producing a virtuous circle of non-inflationary growth.

More pessimistic forecasts argue that the effect of these multipliers is not automatic and that, even in a virtuous circle, winners will only occur if there are losers. Head-on competition in unprotected markets could produce job losses of over half a million a year for a couple of years as the inefficient or the simply unlucky are driven to the wall. Without these resource shifts, none of the multipliers can begin to work. Nor will the new resources necessarily be spread equitably around the EC.

The biggest gains should be felt in those sectors where the barriers have been the most restrictive in the past; that is, in the technologically advanced sectors and among the later arrivals, Greece, Spain and Portugal, whose markets are still the most heavily protected. The smallest gains will probably be in traditional industries, such as footwear, textiles and clothing, in the rich economic heartland where internal barriers have not appeared to impose a severe competitive handicap. The danger, of course, is that the biggest impact will be in the high-tech industries in the heartland which, on picking up momentum, will create a two-speed Europe with France and Germany as the pace-makers, leaving the others further and further behind. It is in this

Mix / Market features	Product	Price	Promotion	Place	Service
Wealth		Is the market rich enough for price not to be a major factor?			
Life style and urbanisation				Where are your outlets located in terms of population centres?	Could you provide the standard of service to which your market is accustomed?
Age structure			At what age group are you targeting promotion?		
Education			What educational level can you assume in your target audience?		
Technology	Has your product a technological edge?				Can the level of technology accommodate your after-sales service requirements?
Competition		How have the prices of your competitors moved in relation to yours in recent years?	How are competing products promoted?		
Market size and market trends		How has the price moved in recent years?			
Market share		How will price affect your market share?			
Retail culture	How are products presented?				
Trade structure		Will more extended channels affect your price?			
Tariffs and non-tariff barriers					

Figure 4.1 *An example of a market profile*

ruthlessly competitive world that you will be increasingly forced to operate. It is essential for you, therefore, to get to know this market and build its rapidly changing parameters into your database.

Market profile

Information on markets needs to be put in a form which allows some comparability. A valuable aid to comparison is a *market profile* for each territory. This is constructed by placing the parameters of your database along two axes: a horizontal one for the elements of the mix and a vertical one for the market features which impact on it. The intersection of the axes provides you with a matrix of cells in which you can locate key questions, a few illustrative examples of which are set out in Figure 4.1. The matrix is not merely a useful *aide-mémoire*. By enclosing the questions in a schematic form, you can run your eye up and down the cells, looking for gaps, searching for connections and generally getting your first overall view of your marketing strategy. In fact, without a comparative format like the one in Figure 4.1 it is difficult even to begin to plan such a strategy.

◀ CHAPTER 5 ▶

MARKET SELECTION

Using your database as a guide, you can now begin your marketing plan by selecting your target markets and deciding how you will position your product to meet competition. This mapping exercise should observe certain operating principles, as follows.

Consumer versus national markets

Consider the map of Europe shown in Figure 5.1. In terms of living standards, it is divisible into two wealthy zones: the Golden Triangle of the North consisting of the home counties of England, northern France, Denmark, the Rhineland and the Benelux countries; and the Golden Sphere of the South consisting of southern Germany, Switzerland, Austria and northern Italy. Each of these areas shares certain cultural affinities and social homogeneities which run across national boundaries. Yet on their fringes lie some of the poorest regions of Europe, in south-eastern France, Yugoslavia and southern Italy. Failure to think in these terms when, for example, marketing high-quality consumer durables could lead to unfortunate errors of targeting, leaving ultimately an agent or a representative stranded in the Vosges when he should have been in Strasbourg or Turin.

Think in terms of consumer rather than national markets.

Market segments

A market segment is a group of buyers with similar purchasing characteristics.

A *market segment* is a group of buyers with similar purchasing characteristics; for example, the West German car market can be

42

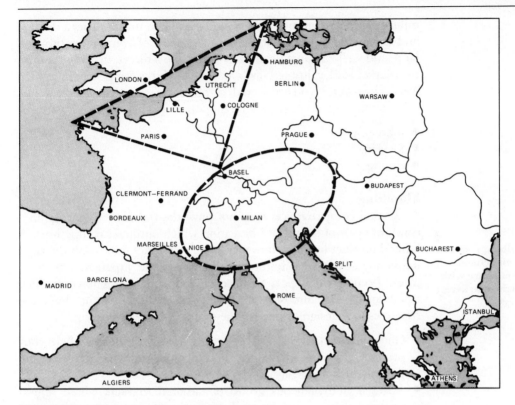

Figure 5.1   *The two wealthy zones of Europe*

divided into an economy segment with strong loyalty in the immediate post-war period to VW, a status segment and a sporting segment. Most markets are a mix of fierce and weak competitive segments, slow and high growth segments. As a rule, the more urbanised a market the more homogeneous its market segments. Put simply, Europe's car workers share more in common than its farm labourers. Segmenting a market can also reveal *strategic windows* for new competitors to challenge established market leaders.

Penetration strategy

Once the mapping exercise is complete and you have decided where and on what basis you intend to compete, you will need to develop a strategy of penetration. In formulating any strategy, two fundamental military principles apply: *objective* and *mass*. You must pursue a definite and attainable objective at the weakest point of your competitors. A large and well-resourced company can make a direct, frontal attack on the market leader, just as Next challenged Marks & Spencer in fashion wear. However, if you are a small company, certain strategic principles are, initially at least, almost forced upon you. These principles are:

- matching
- focusing
- timing.

Matching

As a small company, you may not have the resources to engage in a constant cycle of technical innovation which outflanks competitors. A limited product line can, however, achieve market share with the right marketing strategy. A testament to this are the Japanese who have rarely been technological pioneers and in some cases have avoided technological risk almost as an act of policy. If you do not have the resources to redesign or develop new product lines for export:

A limited product line can achieve market share with the right marketing strategy.

- Choose markets whose characteristics fit those at home, where your product can be sold with little modification, and which have buying points which are easily accessible.
- Select a homogeneous group of national markets whose shared features allow a standardised marketing strategy. An ill-assorted group of markets renders adaptation difficult and creates unnecessary strains on resources.

Focusing

As in selecting markets, so in operating within them, the best strategy for the small company is to select one segment or niche in which it is uniquely able to survive and then develop the marketing mix which meets the specific needs of customers in that segment. If you choose a niche which is peripheral to others' concerns, you can avoid major clashes with your competitors.

Niches often exist in established markets. Exploit them by following a focusing strategy.

Niches often exist in established markets where competitors appear entrenched. In the modern world, it is increasingly rare to find whole countries or even regions where competition in your product line is limited or non-existent. More and more companies are, therefore, following a focusing strategy which outflanks competitors by exploiting niches they have left undefended. Such a strategy brought great success to Japanese audio, hi-fi and motor cycle manufacturers, who first entered narrow market segments and then advanced outwards with a steadily proliferating product range.

Timing

The Japanese were successful because they spread out from their bridgeheads to other segments. A newly discovered profitable niche quickly attracts the interest of predators. It cannot be defended in isolation forever and needs to be reinforced by a policy of progressive penetration which requires you to:

- Begin with a narrow product line which is standardised and cost effective and do not diversify too quickly.
- select your segment as a base and only build outwards as resources permit.
- Begin with the simpler channels of distribution, export houses or importing distributors and gradually move to a firmer base.
- Time both your first entry and later move into other segments. Do not enter before you are ready. Most complaints about British goods overseas are about poor quality and service. It would be unwise, for example, to enter the sophisticated West European market for machinery without good delivery and after-sales service. After all, a good after-sales service can give an otherwise undistinguished product a competitive edge, which places the company in a favourable position for further penetration. At the same time, do not enter too late or stay restricted to your initial segment too long. The worst possible strategy is to signal the existence of your next niche and then leave it unattended.

Time your entry and your move into other segments.

All these strategies have an element of stealth or at least indirectness. They reflect the ancient military maxim that the supreme act of war is to subdue the enemy without fighting. The first move in this war is the pricing of your product. It is to this that we now turn.

◀ CHAPTER 6 ▶

EXPORT PRICING

One of the most difficult problems confronting you in your first venture into the export field is how to price your product. Economic models of pricing exist to help you but most firms ignore them, pricing their goods instead on a purely intuitive understanding of what they 'feel' the market will take. Studies show that in practice, whatever their intuitions about the market, most companies price on the basis of *cost-plus pricing*.

Cost-plus pricing

Price is determined by adding a *mark-up percentage* for a target return on investment to: the *fixed* or *semi-variable* costs of overheads incurred in production, research, selling and promotion; and the *variable* costs of the labour and materials used to produce the goods. In the export field, of course, the mark-up will need to cover the additional costs of shipping documentation, insurance and credit, or the cost of contracting-out facilities.

Cost-plus pricing can be highly standardised by basing your profit percentage on costs incurred in output over a number of years. Cost-plus or standard cost pricing has a number of serious limitations:

● If costs are built into prices on a standard basis, then a reduction in them will bring down the price accordingly. In other words, you get no reward for efficiency. In fact, the reverse will happen. As profit is calculated as a percentage of costs, it too will suffer a reduction.
● If cost-plus pricing puts your price too high, market forces will soon

let you know, but they will not tell you if your price is too low.

- In the export field, you will find variation between markets in prices, distribution costs, tariffs, tax, duties and exchange rate stability. The same cost-plus price may be too high to do business in one market and too low to make a profit in another, which, of course, is an additional reason for following a matching policy and making your first target markets as homogeneous as possible.
- Cost-plus pricing ignores wider profit goals and involves circular reasoning, since price itself influences cost through its effect on sales volume.
- In the final analysis, cost-plus operations provide a useful baseline to measure profitability, but they need to be combined with other more market-oriented strategies. They are particularly dangerous as the sole *modus operandi* in the export field, where markets are so diverse and their impact on profits that much more unpredictable.

Pricing and marketing strategy

Price is, in fact, as we have seen, a component of the marketing mix and should, therefore, be fixed on a marketing rather than a cost basis. A marketing strategy requires, as elsewhere, market information on the relation between the sales and prices of your competitors. You need to study past price movements in relation to volume and see if you can spot the *price leader*, the competitor who is usually the first to move and set a pattern. The price leader is usually the market leader but not always.

Price should be fixed on a marketing rather than a cost basis.

Once you have amassed sufficient data, a number of alternative strategies are available, some of which can be used together. They fall along a continuum with those concerned with short-term gain at one end and those looking to establish a more long-term presence in the export market at the other. We will begin by considering the short-term strategies.

Promotional pricing

This pricing strategy violates price norms to force up sales. It can offer the customer a special reduction in the short term. The motive may be to hold market position, make a windfall in profits, simply clear excess stock or take up the slack in demand out of season. The techniques are:

Promotional pricing violates price norms to force up sales.

Discounting
Discounting is the origin of the 'sales' concept. Nowadays, this has

become an institution in the market with some stores actively buying in for their sales, often from suppliers with special 'sales' lines. This strategy is so successful in shifting large retail sales volume in double-quick time that many stores rely on their sales to trade over the year at a profit.

A special type of psychological discounting exploits the normative expectations of decimal counting by placing the price below the lowest profitable round-digit threshold to achieve an impact, eg £13.99 instead of £14.00.

Discount pricing can become a way of life, with companies permanently setting artificially high prices and then discounting off them on a fairly routine basis. To work effectively, however, discounting requires a pre-existing profile in the market, otherwise the customer cannot assess the significance of the differential and the psychological mechanism cannot begin to work. It is not, therefore, a good option for the market entrant. It can also start a price war, which is why established competitors often use it to dump excess stock beyond their mainstream markets.

Glossing

Glossing sets the price above the going rate to promote the idea of status and prestige on the assumption that, in certain market segments, the price is taken by the customer to be a form of self-evaluation (there is an element of this, of course, in the psychology of all pricing). An example springs to mind.

An ex-colleague of mine once worked for an organisation running courses in 'human relations' for industrial managers. At a meeting held to discuss the low take-up of the courses, a bright spark among the junior management suggested doubling prices. Somewhat surprisingly, this rather reckless idea was adopted on a split vote. Within weeks, the organisation was inundated with applications. For a year or two at least, until the rest of the market caught on, the organisation easily outstripped its low-priced competitors.

Skimming

Skimming uses price differentials for the same product in different markets or market segments to maximise profits. If, for example, you are not too worried about establishing a long-term presence but are after quick profits, you could try pricing more highly in the export market than at home.

Skimming can also be used to exploit very real differences in attitudes to the price of your product in different export markets. In the West German consumer market, price may weigh less with the customer than the quality of service. In the less affluent Portuguese market, the reverse may be the case.

New products generally skim the market at first, bringing in a profit at a low manufacturing level. You can count on your competitors to bring your price down as they copy their way into your market segment.

The effect of skimming is almost always to give you a low and passing market share although, if the product is not a new one, the sudden access of revenue from an export market can counterbalance falls in profitability elsewhere.

As a strategy, skimming always ultimately fails to answer one question: How do you stop other traders equalling up your margins by buying your product in the cheapest market and then undercutting you in the dearest market? Inevitably, the strategy has a limited life span.

Levering

Levering is a subversive form of the kind of *product analysis pricing* used in bidding for a tender. In its most explicit form, product analysis pricing involves the preparation of a pricing data sheet showing the potential buyer the cost of labour, materials etc at market value. In a tender, the sheet will have been prepared to meet the specifications of the buyer and will attempt to fix the lowest quotation compatible with a profit in what is usually a competitive situation. Clearly, the price will be affected by the strength of this competition and how badly you need the order. In levering, the price is fixed as low as possible to land the business and then ratcheted up by 'sudden' discoveries of hidden costs, which can be used to work your margins up afterwards. Who has not suspected themselves to be the victim of this strategy when, for example, a routine item of spot welding on a car's sills develops, at the garage mechanic's sincere insistence, into a major overhaul of the bodywork, doubling or trebling the initial estimated bill? Such is the unfairness of procurement practice in many markets that you may feel ethically free to attempt this manoeuvre.

Penetration pricing

Penetration pricing sacrifices short-term gains for a dominant market share. It is the pricing edge of the policy mentioned earlier, progressive penetration. You pitch your first price below the market range and then increase it in proportion to the growth of your market share. It is a

Penetration pricing sacrifices short-term gains for a dominant market share.

49

common strategy of the Japanese. Of course, the success of the manoeuvre will depend on your having the resources for the long production run needed to reduce unit costs to the point at which profitability will be reached. A large company with spare capacity can follow this path with little risk, but for the small company it requires a lot of nerve. It helps if the product you are exporting has a technological edge, which prevents competitors already entrenched from making an immediate response.

To make sure that you get the volume, you need to cut your prices deep. A small cut will probably reduce your margins with little benefit on sales. Too deep a cut, however, will destabilise the market. You do not want to start a price war.

Successful market penetration requires patience and stealth. You need to take care to avoid an open confrontation; you will sap your competitors' positions. Finally, do not try this strategy too quickly at the top end of the market. It is at the bottom end that customers tend to be most price sensitive.

Whichever of these policies you choose will be determined by your overall market strategy. Failure to incorporate your pricing into this strategy is a serious error of judgement. It could lead to loss of profits or bedevil your attempt to get a long-term presence in the market. Pricing, after all, should never be an afterthought. It is an important component of the marketing mix.

◄ CHAPTER 7 ►

PROMOTION OVERSEAS

The object of promotion is to select the medium which can convey a message; the message is the image of the product which best matches the psychology of the potential buyer. Through the message, the buyer must:

- be made aware of the product's existence;
- perceive the benefits it offers;
- be persuaded it will meet his needs;
- be brought to a state of tension to buy.

The entire sequence involves promotion. An element of the marketing mix, promotion itself is also a further mix of elements which have to be controlled and deployed. These elements are known as the *promotional mix* and include the following:

- *Advertising* involves the placement of advertisements in advertising media at a set rate for the space or time occupied.
- *Publicity* is the release of information to news media in the pursuit of free editorial coverage.
- *Direct marketing* is promotion by telephone, mail or door-to-door contact with the target customers.
- *Forum* is promotion through exhibitions, seminars, fairs or conferences.
- *Sales promotion* is a portmanteau term for gifts, draws, sponsorship, product literature etc.

Promotion can be costly. The answer for small firms on a limited budget is, as with research, to explore the cheapest and most accessible media first. The first step is to determine a small promotional budget on the

Decide which type of medium reaches your target most effectively and economically.

basis of a percentage of projected export sales revenue and then see what possible avenues this budget opens up. The second step is to select the elements of the promotional mix. Decide which type of medium reaches your target audience most effectively and economically.

Advertising

Although advertising is nowadays popularly equated with television advertising, the latter has only about half the share of advertising in general enjoyed by the press, and is considerably more expensive. A limited budget would almost certainly point you in the direction of a *press advertisement*. Your first task is to familiarise yourself with the full range of:

● technical journals
● trade journals
● manufacturers' catalogues
● mail–order catalogues.

You will find a great deal of variation in the spread of technical and consumer magazines across countries. In Western Europe, they are thick on the ground; in the Middle East, they are few and far between. Not to be discounted are English-language publications such as *The Economist* with a global circulation; nor, indeed, the contact sheets sent out by Chambers of Commerce and trade bodies.

Developing copy is a complex and time-consuming affair, which is why over three-quarters of advertising is handled from start to finish by accredited agencies. Less than a quarter of total advertising expenditure is paid direct to the media by do-it-yourself advertisers. However, a limited budget would, again, lead you to take this step. In doing so, follow a simple formula:

● Find the right title from the Department of Trade and Industry's data guide.
● Send for a copy.
● Observe editorial instructions carefully in devising your copy.
● Arrange translation.
● For economy, brief a graphic artist to prepare the artwork.
● Select an agency to do the booking for you.
● Take any advice the agency offers on presentation.

In selecting your agent, choose one with overseas connections or subsidiaries who derives his commission from the publisher. There is a wide choice. In recent years, many native British agencies have developed world-wide connections. Alternatively, you could contact the British representative of the overseas publication directly.

Advertising space does not come cheap. Over £5000 is the page rate for the major German computer magazines.

Publicity

A cheaper method, publicity, can also promote your company overseas if you can find some way of exploiting editorial interest. Such interest is attracted by an innovative product or something unusual about an enterprise. If you have a good story-line, it is best to send it to a number of journals simultaneously. Such stories reach a large audience at low cost and can stimulate not only potential customers but also agents' enthusiasm to handle the product. Reprints provide you with the basis for a small brochure about your product.

The drawback of publicity is one of timing. Waiting lists are often 12 to 18 months and great diversity must be allowed for in editing rules. Sales enquiries from a foreign-language press story generally peak at around three to six months after issue but can filter through for months or even years after. Decide when you want the enquiries and then work backwards to fix the date of the launch.

Alternatively, you could supply the information to the Central Office of Information who, as the government's main publicity organ, send out a constant stream of stories on British exports to newspapers and magazines overseas.

The attraction of this kind of promotion is, of course, its cheapness. Its limitations are transparent. It must constrain the potential customer to draw certain inferences. If it employs a hard sell to get the message across, it soon gets censored. In other words, it needs to be cleverly done. It is also difficult to sustain over time. Few products are sufficiently newsworthy to do this unless they hit a topical theme. Finally, it is very vulnerable to editorial control. What finally emerges on the page may suit the journal's interest rather than your own. The end result is that it rarely, by itself, closes a sale.

Direct marketing

Direct marketing via *direct mail* or *telephone* is the fastest growing sector in

Publicity can promote your company overseas if you can find some way of exploiting editorial interest.

Direct marketing has the advantages of precise targeting and accurate measurement.

53

terms of promotional expenditure. It has the advantages of precise targeting and accurate measurement. In pursuing direct mail, follow a planned formula:

- Locate the market sector.
- Select the class of recipient.
- Compile a list of targets from existing customers *or* contact direct-marketing agents for sources of lists.
- Write copy.
- Pass to a direct-marketing copy-writer for a professional finish.
- Select a percentage of the list and mail.
- Check pilot response.
- Modify approach and mail the balance.

Telephone selling follows essentially the same principles although it has yet to gain a strong footing in the export marketing field.

Forum

Forum includes all those forms of promotion which involve some 'live' theatrical demonstration of the presence of the company in the market-place prior to the act of selling. The 'theatres' which enable you to put your product and company 'on stage' in this way are trade fairs, seminars and conferences.

Exhibiting at trade fairs

Trade fairs provide a useful setting for demonstrating your product/ service, contacting people and carrying out market research.

Foreign trade fairs provide a useful setting for demonstrating products; contacting buyers, agents, wholesalers, retailers and distributors; and also doing, at first hand, some market research. They are particularly valuable in the more planned economies where there are fewer opportunities to meet the customer.

In exhibiting at a fair, certain basic steps apply:

- Obtain a list of exhibitors in preceding years.
- Try to get hold of any lists of visitors in preceding years. If you can buy or rent such a list, you may not need to exhibit at all.
- Keep a record of visitors to your stand.

Successful exhibiting depends on:

Stand presentation
Ensure that your staff know how to set up a stand. A stand needs to be seen as a kind of theatrical presentation in which all the elements 'on stage' are designed not simply to demonstrate the technical aspects of your product but also to dramatise it as a symbol of the collective mission and corporate image of your company, such as 'up market', 'high-tech' or 'environmentally concerned'.

Stand location
Make sure that you have a good central location with enough space to present an imposing foreground. A poor location, out of the way in some far corner or wedged between more commanding competitors, will inevitably reduce the number of visitors to your stand.

Stand administration
Even a good presentation and location cannot compensate for failures in manning: delays in setting up; literature going astray; exhibits lost or late coming; records incomplete or lost during packing; staff unacquainted with important technical details of the product, unable to speak the local language, or just generally unmotivated, leaving the stand unattended for long periods.

Exhibiting is an expensive form of promotion. Its costs incorporate:

- prior research on audience and exhibitors
- design of literature and exhibits
- booking space
- stand construction
- hire of apparatus
- hire of furniture
- samples
- travel and subsistence
- interpreters
- mail
- dismantling
- transport
- storage
- insurance.

Not surprisingly, small exporters are sometimes reluctant to commit their limited resources to such a project in an entirely new market. The Department of Trade and Industry can provide sponsorship.

An alternative, which avoids the costs of participation in an official fair, is to put on an exhibition in a hotel. With sufficient publicity, such ventures can prove lucrative. Can you throw in a small promotional gift as well? Remember the Pirelli calendar? Either way, if these basic steps are carefully observed, there is no more effective way of making a small but solid impact on the local market.

Seminars and conferences

Seminars and conferences are a useful promotional forum particularly for companies in the fields of service and technology. Such events are much used by operators in, for example, pharmaceuticals and international tourism.

Sales promotion

Sales promotion includes such elements as premium offers, price cuts, gifts, prize draws and competitions, sponsorship, product literature and so on. Much used on the home market, they are difficult for the small firm to operate abroad.

Personal selling

As a final promotional tool in the marketing mix, we must include the act of personal selling, which allows the representative to test the selling proposal before closing the deal. An important factor in successful selling is knowing the local business etiquette:

- correct modes of address
- body language
- rules of speech and silence
- food and drink
- language.

The cultural barriers that have to be overcome in each of these areas will be discussed in the next chapter where we deal with the aspects of selling that relate to distribution. For the moment, however, just a cautionary word about language.

The language of the customer

In all forms of sales promotion overseas, try to use the customer's language. English is a commercial lingua franca but fluent speakers of English still prefer to do business in their own language. At a trade fair, for example, visitors will expect to find both literature and presenters who can speak to them in their own language. Similarly, if you send literature abroad by direct mail or other media, it will only be effective if expressed in the language of the readers. The same principle applies to all forms of public relations. If you have a newsworthy innovative product that you want to feature in a foreign journal, remember that most do not publish in English. If you send a foreign editor an English text, he has to get it translated before publishing it. Translated texts have a better chance of publication in technical journals.

> **In all forms of sales promotion overseas, try to use the customer's language.**

Make sure that texts for translation are not idiomatic. Idioms often do not survive translation into other languages. If the text is technical, it should be carefully checked. Even one technical error can destroy credibility. Ensure that translators have a technical understanding of the product or service. Remember also that languages differ in their economies of information processing and use up different amounts of copy space: Spanish, for example, takes 20 to 25 per cent more words than English to express the same concept.

Finally, it is worth remembering that poor linguistic command creates a bad image – a lack of professionalism. After all, the audience will think, if the firm cannot communicate effectively, what is the rest of its service going to be like?

Awareness of these factors has led to a number of government-inspired initiatives in recent years to stimulate the interest of employers in foreign-language learning as a part of staff development. The response of some managing directors has been uninformed but energetic. It often takes the following form: sales staff are directed to find a holiday language course at a local evening institute. The issue of such a directive generally closes the affair as far as the management is concerned. Yet the response of most companies to more systematic offers of staff development is baffling to say the least. Recently, a British Chamber of Commerce circularised 3000 companies, offering courses in business French. It received three replies.

Promotion in general

Whichever elements of the mix you use, timing is very important. At least some material should precede your entry into a market-place, but not too early or the impact will be lost.

Remember also that the cheapest and probably the best promotion, over the long term, is by word of mouth. It can account for up to a quarter of new adopters of products. Much ink has been spilled over the question of the minimal level of awareness at which word of mouth begins to take off. Almost certainly, quality, finish and after-sales service are powerful factors in reaching that threshold. Bear in mind also that consumer research has found that bad news does indeed travel faster than good. The old adage is true, which is yet another reason for carefully timing your entry into the market.

◄ CHAPTER 8 ►

DISTRIBUTION

Once you have fixed your price as part of your marketing strategy and used your promotional budget as best you can to signal your presence in the market, your next step is to plan how to get your goods to your potential customers. In other words, you must select your *channels of distribution*. Decisions in this area are important because they intimately affect all other choices in the marketing mix and, once made, cannot be easily changed. Essentially, the choices you must make concern *selling points* and *transportation*.

Selling points

The critical choice is between *direct selling* with or without an agent who will act on your behalf and *indirect selling* via one or more intermediaries who may, indeed, hold and distribute the stock on their own account. You will already have made this decision once before when you first entered the home market. Now the context is different. New channels of distribution encountered overseas may mean that you will have to make new distinctions between *customer* and *consumer*. The customer may be part of an extensive resale chain which ends in a consumer far removed from the original purchase; a factor not to be overlooked in the presentation of your product as it inevitably determines to whom you should direct your major selling effort.

Moreover, channels of distribution change. Like products they have a life cycle. Yesterday's forms give way to new ones more geared to today's markets. In France, small stores and supermarkets have lost ground to large hypermarkets on the edge of conurbations. In Germany, mail-order firms which grew apace in the seventies tended to stagnate in the eighties. Not all such developments will have convenient parallels in your own sector of the home market. You need, therefore, to keep abreast of events, which underscores yet again the importance of market research prior to entry.

In general, exporters tend to use intermediaries in the following situations:

- Where resources are low and the exporter has too thin a cash flow to meet heavy haulage costs, stock losses or trade debts.
- Where the size of the orders is difficult because orders are either too small or dispersed in space or time, or too big to handle directly.
- Where the product is standardised and highly saleable and little is, therefore, required of the seller in the way of specialist knowledge or promotion.
- Where the exporter is unacquainted with local wholesale and retail markets.

When any one of these factors changes, when resources improve, turnover grows, the orders come through in a more manageable size, the product itself begins to require more promotional support or you yourself simply become more familiar with the overseas markets, you will begin to feel a pressure to shift from *indirect* to more *direct* forms of distribution according to the following sequence, with the ultimate preference usually being an overseas base, where this is economically feasible:

- export house
- distributor
- collaborator
- agent
- representative
- overseas base.

Research has found that a gradual penetration which progresses through this sequence as business builds is indeed the key to success.

The particular stage at which you enter this sequence will also depend very much on the nature of your product. Different sectors of the market have their own tradition, and, of course, the sequence is a generalisation which covers a multitude of modes of operation. The activities of many firms would defy any attempt to locate a cut-off point which could define the stage of distribution they have reached. Many, for example, combine an agent and a representative operating in, more or less, the same territory. Nevertheless, as a broad description of a general trend this sequence holds true.

Indirect selling

If you decide to use an intermediary you should seek one that satisfies the following three criteria. The intermediary should:

An intermediary reduces the element of risk.

- be oriented to serving the target market;
- have the requisite technical and other resources to help exploit your competitive advantage;
- be as controllable as possible.

The role of an intermediary is to reduce the element of risk, which is why this path is so often chosen by the first-time exporter. The least risky of all bridges to the export market is the long established system of using an *export house*.

Export houses

Of these, nearly 800 in the UK handle about 28 per cent of the country's export trade. Although they tend to specialise in particular categories of merchandise for particular countries, they are usually strongest in English-speaking markets and in the field of consumer rather than industrial goods. They have three modes of operation:

Export merchants. In effect, export merchants operate as just another UK customer up to the point of sale, buying and holding stock and taking total responsibility thereafter for pricing, promotion, distribution and shipping. Export houses of this kind offer by far the safest route into the export market. The cost to you, the supplier, of course, is complete loss of marketing control at the point of hand-over. The price you receive will also have to reflect the export house's need to cover its own costs.

Export agents. Export agents operate simply as agents, virtually a *de facto* export department for you, the supplier, who remain as principal throughout, guaranteeing delivery and setting the price but leaving the export house to handle selling and documentation, and sometimes also forwarding and after-sales service. The price charged will vary according to the extent of the service and may include a commission on sales.

Buying and confirming agents. Buying and confirming agents find sources of supply for an overseas buyer or deal with suppliers nominated by the buyer, paying cash for the goods and arranging shipping on the buyer's behalf. You, the supplier, receive a 'confirmation' or virtual guarantee of the overseas order and, more important, payment from the confirmer on shipment without recourse to compensation for buyer default. Some overseas principals have their own buyers resident in the UK, often operating from their own wholly owned buying offices, especially in the retail consumer field. Although not always empowered to buy new products, they can provide an influential route to their principals. Buying offices of American department stores, in particular, can provide a useful first route into the lucrative North American market. A list of such buying offices is available from the DTI.

The logic of using an export house follows the rules for using intermediaries in general. For all practical purposes, an export house can be considered as just another UK customer, but one who relieves the supplier of the routine work and credit risks in overseas transactions. Risks to the supplier are minimal, which is why export houses are such an attractive proposition for the small first-time exporter. In fact, the more limited your manpower and financial resources, the more attractive they become. Remember that, if a buyer defaults, the Export Credits Guarantee Department (ECGD) will pay you less than the full cover on a short-term contract and then only after time taken to verify the claim, whereas if you use a confirming house you bear none of the risk of default and receive the full amount for your goods on shipment. You do, of course, lose control of marketing but, if you are a first-time exporter, your turnover may be low and dispersed among a number of markets, none of which is of a scale to justify an independent marketing operation. Anyway, even if the market is growing the orders may come in too soon for you to have developed effective export marketing skills.

Much depends on the nature of the product. Export houses are notoriously conservative. They deal most happily with what they can be certain to dispose of. It is not always easy to get them to handle a new product. New products require careful promotion. If you want your product to enter the export market with a special brand image, you must ask yourself whether it is wise to relinquish all control of its marketing once it has left your premises.

Fortunately, export houses do not exhaust the possibilities of low-risk entry into the export market. Another intermediary who plays the role of your customer but this time from an overseas base is an *importing distributor*.

Importing distributors

Importing distributors buy and take title to your goods and then sell them either direct to the consumer or to the different channels of distribution. The profit for the distributor lies in the margin between the cost of the goods delivered to the overseas warehouse and the price at which they can be resold to retail, wholesale or other outlets. Generally, a distributor acts as the sole channel for supply to a specified territory. In some cases, the role of the distributor shades into that of an agent. This is particularly so where the distributor seeks to hold stocks on consignment, but in such a case the stocks remain the property of you, the supplier, until they are sold. Unfortunately, you must then bear the costs of storage and insurance, and run the risk of shrinkage or loss from damage or theft.

Holding stock in this way inevitably reduces the incentive of distributors to shift the goods as rapidly as possible. When they do so, however, they usually have the advantage of good specialist knowledge of the local wholesale and retail trade, and provide a good first avenue into it for the new exporter. A disadvantage is that, as in the case of using an export house, you tend to lose touch with your ultimate consumers. This makes it more difficult to replace the distributor in the course of time with a more direct line of contact with the market. As with an export house, loss of control over the marketing of the product leaves it unprotected from the vagaries of the local market. If you are selling plastic buckets this may be no great loss, but if your product is more complex and innovative you may seek to protect its image by signing an agreement of exclusive distribution, which channels it only through certain favoured outlets.

In general, distributors are most useful when their skills of low-cost contact, service and storage are more important than their lack of commitment to the brand, and when there is little hope of developing customer loyalty. They do bear some risk, however, and are proportionately more intolerant of a slow-selling start. Thus, they are often reluctant to accept entirely new product lines. The best proof of your potential in this regard is a list of orders already taken through other sources.

Despite the popularity of distributors in many sectors of the market, a surprisingly large number of companies trade overseas through different types of *collaborative arrangement*.

Collaborators
The different types of collaborative arrangement are:

Supplying to a large exporter. This is the safest form of collaborative entry into an export market. Indeed, many of the products of small companies find their way abroad in this form through the supply of components to other UK manufacturers. Companies making car accessories, for example, often find their markets in this way.

Subcontracting. A number of UK companies are engaged in large-scale overseas operations for which they require secondary suppliers. If yours is a small company in the civil engineering field, for example, you can scan the trade journals for imminent tenders and then move in with an offer to supply.

Crown Agents. These are a public service operating for principals in public sectors overseas and inviting tenders for products or projects. They have a large remit as buyers and pay the suppliers in the UK. Other public sector concerns which can often provide a useful source of orders, even for small companies, are international agencies like the United Nations and the World Health Organisation. Have you ever thought of the unimaginable openings that such large bureaucracies offer, for example, to suppliers of office furniture?

Joint marketing. If your product is novel and the costs of distribution are high, you could seek collaboration with a larger UK company which has an overseas marketing organisation. The larger company may have an overseas subsidiary with a gap you could fill in its product line.

Reciprocal collaboration. As a variant of the preceding arrangement, you might consider a reciprocal agreement with a foreign company, allowing each of you to sell the other's products in your home market. One advantage of this arrangement over more conventional forms of distribution is that it reduces competition for marketing attention from potentially hostile product lines. If you are interested in such an arrangement, you need to keep an eye on possible avenues of approach. Foreign companies seeking a UK collaborator frequently appear in the circulars of local Chambers of Commerce.

Consortia. These are groups of manufacturers or suppliers of a service who together open up an opportunity overseas. The DTI can sometimes operate as a facilitator in these schemes. With increasing European integration, more companies will be seeking an overseas partner. If you are interested in finding such a partner, then there are a number of paths along which you can proceed. You can:

- talk to suppliers, distributors or banks;
- advertise in a foreign trade journal;
- use the marriage bureau services of the European Commission's Business Co-operation Network (BC-Net), an organisation specifically set up to help companies in the European Community to find a business partner.

Licensing. This is not necessarily an export process but it does allow a company with technical know-how or an innovative product to establish a market presence overseas by granting the licensee the right to use its knowledge or patents in the manufacturing process. After all, selling rights is a useful source of income and a legitimate activity in the export drive. It is a useful alternative if entry to the market is beyond your reach because of cost or other barriers. The attendant risks you run are those which always menace the merchandiser of intellectual property to companies which can use it to become potential competitors. A form of licensing is called *franchising*, in which the licensee not only pays the licence fees but also contributes to resources. In return, the franchisor usually provides assistance in marketing the product or service.

Direct selling

Via an agent

Direct selling via an agent is often the recourse of the first-time exporter. The ultimate purpose of selecting an agent should be, as the first step in a long-term strategy, to develop a permanent presence in the overseas market. Unlike importing distributors, agents do not take title to their stock; nor, unless they are 'del credere' agents, do they normally take responsibility for credit risks. What they offer you, the exporter, is, in the absence of anything better, at least a physical presence in the market, which could be crucial to your custom if service or spare parts are likely to be needed.

The disadvantage of using agents is that, at a distance, they cannot be easily controlled or even stimulated to do much in the way of selling and

The ultimate purpose of an agent is to develop a permanent presence in the overseas market.

65

promotion if they do not feel so inclined. If, through lack of marketing, turnover falls, they will often simply concentrate on their more profitable lines. Nor, in such circumstances, are they always easy to sever. You will need to familiarise yourself with the small print which defines the legal status of different types of agent in your target market. There is, in fact, an extraordinary variety of different types: at least 27 according to a recent estimate. At one end of the scale are those who merely take orders and earn commission on the number of sales; at the other are those who take responsibility for all aspects of sales promotion from advertising to after-sales service. Clearly, agents with this wider brief are unlikely to be satisfied with simple payment by commission.

Payment by commission is itself a double-edged sword. It tends to produce a selling rather than a marketing orientation. Motivated by the immediate reward of a commission, the agent may shift stock at great speed without any thought for long-term strategy. The consequence for you may be a flow of defaulters and transient customers, which will never give you a firm base in the market. Payment by commission can lead the agent to see you not as someone with a long-term market strategy in mind but as just another customer to whom orders are sold for a commission.

In fact, the interests of agent and principal never completely coincide. Most agents have a number of principals and what they usually seek is a stable turnover for a minimum of effort which guarantees a certain level of commission from all of them. This is not quite what you, as a principal, have in mind when you appoint them. In some countries, however, the tradition is such that it is difficult to avoid using them. In **Agents are most used in markets where the trade structure is poor and the product is sales led.** West Germany, for example, two-thirds of the import trade passes through their hands. In other countries, they are not quite so predominant. As a rule, you do best to use them in all markets where the trade structure is rudimentary or poor and the product itself is sales led, needing little in the way of marketing and customer service.

How to find the right agent is one of the first questions to perplex the first-time exporter. In fact, both agents and distributors can be located in a number of sources. A number of options are open to you. You can:

- contact the DTI;
- ask existing suppliers;
- advertise in the foreign trade press;
- attend overseas trade fairs;
- use the DTI's Export Initiative.

The problems involved in contacting, selecting and then controlling agents are best discussed under the two broad headings of recruitment and management.

Recruitment. The first priority should be to draw up a job description. This should specify:

Recruitment. Draw up a job description for the agent.

- requisite experience
- technical knowledge
- area of operation
- lines carried
- financial standing
- terms of payment.

After compiling as large a list as possible from your sources, you should then write to each agent, stating your requirements and asking for as much information as possible in return. From the replies, you can then make a short list of candidates for you to visit personally in search of answers to a number of questions. You need to ask whether they have:

- the resources to cover the target market;
- the technical knowledge to handle the product;
- sufficient experience of working in the market;
- a good track record in similar product lines;
- any competing lines in their existing portfolio;
- too many principals already to allow much time for you.

If the agent is already operating, a visit should be made to observe his daily round of work.

Once again, you could do worse than follow the example of the Japanese, who take enormous care in appointing their agents. They at least realise the importance of this first step in the strategy of achieving a long-term base in the market. Not only must you try to observe your agents at work and get a good look at their facilities, you must also examine very closely their contractual status. How much protection do they enjoy in local agency legislation? In some countries, once appointed, they are hard to remove. Could a trial period be built into the contract? It is the careful and unhurried attention to such questions which has brought the Japanese so much success in their use of agents overseas.

Caution is particularly advisable at the contractual stage. The International Chamber of Commerce has produced a useful publication entitled *Guide for Preparing Agent Contracts between Parties from Different*

Countries. A number of different types of contract can be envisaged depending on the type of agency. Any contract should cover the following areas:

- name and principal office of each party
- earnest of intent in each other's best interests
- the product line covered by the terms
- the territory to which the agreement applies
- an exclusion clause against selling beyond the territory specified
- the exclusivity or otherwise of the agency relation
- the mode of operation of the agent
- the promotional obligations of the parties concerned
- exclusion from the agent's competency of conflicting product lines
- safeguards for the product under international trade mark and patent legislation
- conditions of stockholding
- commitment of the parties to after-sales service
- training requirements
- commission and methods of payment
- agent responsibility in meeting claims and guarantees
- duration of the agreement
- terms of renewal, termination or expiry
- terms of arbitration.

In the first instance, it is advisable to appoint an agent to a territory that is small enough for your initially limited resources to be able to support.

As far as the price of your product is concerned, you may, especially if the market is highly competitive, wish to allow certain margins of price within which your agent can operate. Do not allow too much leeway or your prices could start to go haywire and wreck any long-term strategy.

By the way, it is the custom for agents to be paid commission on all orders coming out of their territory even if these have gone direct from the customer to you without, as far as you know, the agent having had any hand in them.

Remember also to set a sales target and make it a reasonably high one. Monitor sales performance closely and give a good bonus for reaching the target.

Management. Keep in touch with your agent.

Management. The most important part of managing agents is keeping them in the picture. From conversations I have had recently with British exporters, it is clear that not much more than a third had visited any of their agents in the past year or so. Keeping in touch with an agent is essential where business transactions require technical assistance. But there are other reasons for doing so.

Most agents, as we have noted, handle the goods of a number of principals. As a rule, however, the principal who pays the agent the most attention generally gets the best results.

Visiting alone is of little use unless motivated by specific objectives. On this score, it is best to arrange the visit well in advance. Lightning visits create suspicion and resentment, and can miss the mark completely if the 'focus' of the visit happens to be very busy at that point or, worse, is away on business.

Agents themselves vary in the degree of support they feel they need. Some are constantly on the phone, while others are only contactable in a crisis.

Planning before a visit always pays dividends. Check over the sales record of the agent beforehand and try to familiarise yourself with those features of the market which could help in discussions to show that you understand some of the workaday problems of selling the products in that locality. Without some knowledge of this kind, you can hardly claim to be offering a supportive role, and your visit will come to look more and more like an act of surveillance. Always try to bring some new technical or commercial sales literature with you. Finally, arrange an itinerary which enables you to spend at least a day or two with the agent on his rounds. You need to learn as much as you can about your agent's selling routine. Without making it look too much like a policing operation, run through a checklist of questions which need to be answered about the agent's performance. You need to ask:

- How many customers have renewed their orders recently?
- Has the agent acquired any new principals?
- What, if any, new promotions have been started?
- What is the agent's attitude to your product?
- Does the agent appear to need any new training?
- Could you offer more practical support to the sales drive?
- What areas of the market are being left uncovered and why?
- What reasons does your agent offer for failure to achieve any sales targets?
- Have you heard them before from others? If so, they are probably valid.

Above all, try to see the agent in operation with a prospective customer. Watch for any weaknesses in selling style. The more you know about the local market situation the better. Your agent will tend to exaggerate the difficulties of selling in the local market to justify his sales record. In turn, temper your observations with encouragement. It is not always easy but try to find something to praise.

Take the agent into your confidence. Air your thoughts about the future of the company. Discuss sales strategy and development of new lines. Ask for advice on possible technical modifications which might increase sales.

Again, language skills are at a premium. Even if your agent has a good command of English, showing that you have a passing acquaintance with his language makes you look less manipulable. Even a little phrase-book knowledge of the language is a help.

Where more than one agent is appointed, it is often useful to send out an occasional news-letter, informing agents in the field of recent company developments.

The key to good customer relations is never to lose touch but to keep your company constantly in the client's mind; in this respect, your agent is to you a kind of customer to whom the image, idea, mission or whatever you like to call it, of your company must be sold. Following through this general principle of keeping the channels constantly open, make sure that all correspondence from the agent is answered as rapidly as possible. Finally, give immediate technical and back-up services as soon as they are required.

Via a representative
Opting to dispense with an agent and to go for a more direct link with the market involves a lot of preparatory work. This is particularly so if the agent has been allowed a completely free hand. If you have not kept in close touch, you will have lost the opportunity to learn about the market under your agent's unwitting tutelage and you will need to set to and:

- investigate the local trade structure for yourself;
- identify buying points;
- find out in detail about buying procedures.

Agents, once assigned a territory, are generally left to distribute their activities within it as they see fit. Greater accountability is expected of a company's own sales force. Travel and subsistence costs now become a direct charge to you, the supplier, and you will want not only to delimit the sales territory to manageable and cost-effective proportions but also to split it up into segments which allow key customers to be visited on a regular basis without too much loss of time and money.

The decision to dispense with an agent or distributor usually follows some change in turnover which suggests that a representative on the spot could generate extra sales. These sales are not likely to come immediately, which means that the extra cost will have to be borne for a while. Yet, at this stage, cost itself should not be the major factor in decision-making. If you have a reasonably sized sales force, having one of your representatives based in Europe for six months of the year is not going to be that much more expensive than having him travelling around your home market in the same period.

Big expense always comes with the setting up of an overseas sales base. Overriding any consideration of costs at this stage is usually the desire for greater control of the local operation. But that control will be wasted without proper training. If you already have an overseas agent or distributor and would like to dispense with him but do not yet feel confident of the ability of any of your present staff to replace him, you could, as a first step, get one of your staff to work alongside him, thereby exploiting any profitable existing arrangements and getting some useful on-the-job training into the bargain. If you try this ploy, however, you cannot easily prevent your agent spotting its implications. The more successful this collaboration, the more quickly he will realise that he is doing himself out of a job. Whatever the interim arrangement, however, you cannot ultimately dodge this issue of specific sales training for the overseas market. Your representatives will need to know:

Who to sell to. They will need to know the different trade structures of the overseas market and any novel features in the type of customer they are likely to confront.

What to sell. No one sells a product. What you sell is the perceived benefits it brings to the satisfaction of the customer's needs. These needs may be different in the overseas market. You may, for example, be used to selling your product on the basis of its quality finish, but in a less affluent market, price competitiveness may be a better seller.

Where to sell. The locale of business deals may be very different in the overseas market. Business can be done in a Spanish cafe, for example, which no Scandinavian could imagine occurring beyond the office door.

Do not be misled by appearances. In Britain, we tend to associate size, space and gloss with status. The correlation does not necessarily hold abroad. We expect the chairman of the board to have the biggest office, but the French think of office space and location less in terms of status than in terms of centrality to a perceived network of influence. A French director will often have his office in the middle of his subordinates, where he can control them. In Latin America or the Middle East, the outer appearance of a building may look appallingly run-down. Do not imagine that this reflects as badly on the status of its occupants as the same condition of a building might do in the UK. Different norms apply and the status of a business is judged by other things.

How to sell. This is the area where cultural differences are sharpest and where the greatest pitfalls await the exporter. It is not simply a matter of learning foreign languages. People do tend to prefer to buy in their own language even if they sell in English. Yet many are happy to practise their skills in what is, after all, the world's commercial 'lingua franca' and the spread of English in this role ensures an increasing number of people with such an attitude of mind. The real problem for the direct seller abroad, whether operating in an English language or a foreign language context, is to understand 'the culture'; that is, the particular codes of understanding that are so deeply embedded that their native users are virtually unaware of them. This is the area of what is called *communicative competence* and Japanese companies believe it to be so important that many of them put their executives through a three-month training programme, involving much role-playing and simulation, before sending them abroad. To organise such a programme, a lot of prior research is required.

The costs of this kind of staff development are obviously prohibitive for the small exporter. What you can do instead is to glean as much data as you can on the business culture of the market from libraries, exploratory visits of your own or the second-hand accounts of others and then feed the information into a short programme of staff development, perhaps in the form of a series of weekend seminars. It sounds a tiresome exercise but it is precisely the lack of systematic training in this area which has led to so much failure in the past. This is truly an area in which a little knowledge does go a long way. Here is a list of the features of the host business culture where differences are most likely to occur:

Your representative needs to be aware of the features of the host business culture.

Attitudes to time. It is difficult to realise just how different attitudes to time are in other cultures. To European business men, tight schedules and the mobility which often accompanies them are taken as a first-line sign of the power, status and efficiency of the operative. An opposite number with an empty and endlessly accommodating diary arouses suspicion. We expect a flourishing concern to be short of time and to set limits on any encounter with us. The expectation is often quite otherwise in an Asian or Middle Eastern country. To give a prior deadline or to put a guillotine on a discussion may be seen as quite insulting to an Arab. To us in the West, however, 'time kept waiting' is a measure of status. Subordinates are kept waiting by their superiors and they would not dream of reversing the relationship. If we are kept waiting for appointment in an outer office, we take this as a downgrading in status or a measure of the indifference of our opposite number. In Latin America, attitudes are different. To be kept waiting for an hour is of little significance.

The same attitude often applies to correspondence. A delay of a month or two in a reply from a Japanese business man does not necessarily mean any loss of interest. On the contrary, it is often a sign that your proposition has been thoroughly investigated from every angle.

The underlying factor would seem to be a difference between cultures in the value placed on different time spans. We tend to think in terms of short spans. Five minutes is a common unit. If you are five minutes late for a meeting you will probably give a full apology; if you are 10 or 15 minutes late, you almost certainly will. For a Levantine Arab, the smallest, significant unit is longer, perhaps 15 minutes at least. An Arab arriving 10 minutes late would, therefore, not think that he had significantly delayed the encounter and so would not dream of giving a full apology. Half an hour's delay would be significant for him as well as for you, in which case he might well do so. The moral of the story is clear. Do not assume that long delays abroad necessarily mean that you are not getting anywhere.

Greetings, leave-taking and forms of address. Each culture has its own rules for beginning and ending an interaction and addressing people within it. In the Middle East, for example, in casual encounters, men almost always shake hands on meeting, chat for a few minutes and then shake hands on leaving. A second encounter on the same day would follow the same sequence. In Britain, we tend to shake hands less and certainly so on the second encounter. We also tend to shake hands and then stand back. Latin Americans stand their ground, a stance which a number of my business friends have found quite intimidating.

Speaking the host language opens up the further problem of how to address people. In Britain, we tend to use surnames first and then move rapidly to Christian names as a sign that we feel the relationship is 'warming up'. In many languages, the same thermostatic control is operated through the pronoun system, with two words for 'you', one familiar and the other socially more distant. Because we have lost this distinction in the demise of our old pronoun 'thou', we tend to forget it, much to our cost in certain countries. The use of the more distant 'vous' is *de rigueur* in French business circles. Loquacious the French may be but, socially, they are very reserved. A premature shift to the familiar 'tu' will irritate your French negotiator. The same formality extends to the use of Christian names. It may surprise you to know that a French director of even quite a small firm will often not know the Christian names of most of his staff. The moral here is not to take the initiative in signalling greater 'warmth' in the relationship but to simply wait for your opposite number to give the cue.

Ground rules. As important as fluency in a language is knowing the rules of behaviour which determine how people relate to each other in a business setting. You need to know, for example, what it is permissible to raise as a topic of casual conversation in the 'warm-up' to the actual negotiation. A Frenchman, for example, would be acutely embarrassed if you raised the issue of the financial status of his company; a Canadian would not think twice about it.

On personal matters, cultural differences are even more pronounced. A direct 'How are the wife and kids?' in front of strangers would petrify an Arab. An American response would be entirely different.

Even voice levels are a factor. Arabs are often surprised by the low voice levels of British speakers, levels which are indicative for them of weakness. British speakers will only raise their voice levels to convey emphasis or emotion. This is not so in other cultures. A speaker of Indian English will speak louder not because he feels strongly about the issue but merely to keep the floor and resist interruption.

In any negotiation, speech alternates with silence as the concept of the business deal develops between the parties. The longer the silence the more strenuous it is for the Western negotiator. Other cultures have a greater tolerance. In Japan, meetings proceed through frequent pauses for reflection and appraisal. These silences are often given a sinister interpretation by Western business men, who then fill them with an offer of a price cut or otherwise weaken their position. At least one Japanese business man has told me that he now deliberately prolongs his silences to exert stronger pressure for a better deal.

Too often in sales training, we emphasise how to talk and forget that there are skills involved in knowing how to listen. These skills also vary widely across different cultural settings. A New Yorker will punctuate your speech with enthusiastic pause-fillers which urge you to proceed: 'no kidding?', 'sure', 'no way'. A similar involvement would receive only a sage nod from a Japanese. As critical to the outcome of a deal is how to interpret 'yes' and 'no'. Polite Japanese never say 'no'. You must understand from how they say 'yes' whether or not they mean it. In fact, you will encounter enormous cultural variations in how 'no' is signalled around the world. You will encounter 'silence', offers to postpone decision-making, shift of responsibility to a third party over whom the buyer has no control, willing acceptance in principle but with a reluctance to discuss any details, and a host of diversionary or distracting tactics.

Speech and silence provide a surprisingly limited set of signals. It has been suggested that up to two-thirds of information is conveyed by other means. Take how you sit, for instance. You may not know that even this can create an impression bad enough to make your opposite number ill at ease in your presence and, therefore, mentally unprepared to close the deal. Arabs sit closer to each other than we do. On a sofa or divan, they prefer to sit alongside and then turn and speak quite closely and directly to you. A European's first inclination is to back off from such a close encounter. In close encounters of this kind, the French tend to react most formally. The Americans often go to the other extreme. To convey a sense of informality in his own office, an American may put his feet up on the desk. The soles of the feet displayed in this way are a threatening taboo area to an Arab, who will immediately back away.

In fact, directness is less important to an Arab than steadiness of gaze. Lack of eye contact passes in the Middle East for slyness, disrespect or inattention. More than one Arab business man has told me that he finds it near impossible to do a deal with someone wearing sun-glasses. One actually claimed to have said to a European: 'Please, take off your sun-glasses so that I can talk to you.' Yet the same amount of contact would be quite menacing to a Japanese. In Britain, we tend to maintain our gaze when listening and disperse it when speaking. The opposite applies throughout the African continent. Africans break their gaze when listening but maintain a steady gaze as soon as they begin to speak, a reaction which can seem quite domineering and aggressive to a western business man.

Equally threatening, at least to the British, is the constant touching that foreigners use to keep themselves on the same wavelength in discussion. As a rule, the Arabs touch more than the southern Europeans, the southern Europeans more than the Americans, the Americans more than us. Touch conveys warmth. So does food. In the Middle East, a business visit is unheard of without the offer of refreshment. Do not be misled by the Arab's refusal of any food you offer. In much of the Arab world it is polite, even if one is hungry, to refuse food the first or second time it is offered, although a third refusal is taken to be definitive.

Even the words 'thank you' are not always what they seem. In France, 'merci' generally means 'no thank you'; in the US, 'thanks' means the opposite, 'yes, thanks'.

Food is a gift. There are others. Beware of accepting them. There is an old Arab saying: 'Please do not be grateful; you will repay me.'

Rules of negotiation. Finally, the most important set of rules are those that determine how the negotiations are conducted. Take the contract itself. The British tend to consider that negotiations have ceased when the contract is signed. Any attempt to renege on the deal is sought in the fine print of the contract and is ultimately a matter for the courts to decide. To the Greek business man, the contract appears in a quite different light. It is merely one stage on the route to negotiation which will only cease when the goods are delivered or the work is complete. It is, in fact, the contractual basis for serious negotiation.

In many countries, a contract is seen as a manoeuvre in an overall strategy which begins with an opening gambit. The first moves in this game reveal wide variations in the scope you are allowed as a player. Italians allow a lot of scope for manoeuvre from the beginning. The Scandinavians operate with a much tighter margin. The Chinese begin, after careful reflection, with what they feel is an equitable arrangement and then tend to stick stubbornly to it.

Once negotiations have begun, their phases and sequencing vary widely. Arabs have a cyclical form of argumentation in which they constantly spiral out to what seem like irrelevances before returning endlessly to the same point. The French proceed more logically and schematically, building from particulars to what they conceive to be their general point.

In any deal, the mention of price and the possibility of discounting is a critical point. In Latin America, do not mention the price until you are asked. In the UK, the seller tends to take the initiative. In Latin America, the buyer likes to be the one who gives the signal. Ultimately, of course, the question of price must be raised. At this point, your Arab buyer may suddenly react quite violently, claiming to have been misled and threatening to break off negotiations there and then. If you have a margin in which to operate, do not reduce too early. The reaction is a ploy. He may be only testing prices with you, before buying the goods from one of your competitors.

On the whole, bargaining favours the buyer. The only advice which can be offered is to decide your margins beforehand and then to move between them only under the strongest pressure. If you are too volatile yourself, you will disappoint your Arab buyer. He expects a struggle and one conducted according to the strict rules of bargaining etiquette.

Do not expect too direct a response. In Asia and the Middle East, we confront what sociologists call a 'shame' culture. It is vitally important that no one loses face. This applies as much to you as to the buyer. This is why an Arab will often give you promises he cannot keep. He does not want to give offence; otherwise, you will lose face. Remember also that, evasive though they are in tactics, the Arabs are accustomed to exaggeration in expression. A neutral 'yes' from an Arab buyer may seem positive to you but to him it may mean little more than a polite diversion. A stronger, positive commitment from an Arab would be given a much more powerful mode of expression.

Finally, do not be too impatient to close the deal. In the Middle East, business discussions are expected to be conducted graciously, at a gentle, leisurely pace with occasional stops for casual conversation and refreshment. This reflects a general attitude quite common in other parts of the world. A business transaction is a social transaction. People expect to get to know you at a personal level. Trust is a matter for mutual negotiation and not, as we tend to feel, something reflected immediately in our credentials. In his negotiations with Arab leaders, Kissinger used to spend hours ensconced with them in small talk, swapping personal intimacies. He felt this tactic to be a sound investment. To us, it seems unbusinesslike and ultimately unrealistic because we distinguish carefully between friendship and clientage. It is hard to imagine the blurring of these boundaries without a cost to professionalism. Yet the same

THE NEW EXPORT MARKETER

attitude extends to the Japanese, the great success story of our era. They do not, any more than the Arabs, make a distinction between business and polite, social exchange. For them, negotiation is total involvement with the other party. This is the attitude which we saw earlier reflected in their use of agents.

Throughout much of the world, the wheels of business are oiled by a friendship which implies definite commercial obligations. You will find that a network of friends is essential as the only sound foundation for a long-term business presence in many overseas markets.

The cultural differences outlined are no more than illustrations of the kinds of difference which will confront you or your personnel overseas. Given such problems of staff development, it is not surprising that few small exporters ever choose this route to the overseas market. One hears cases of managing directors themselves driving abroad with a bootful of samples and doing the rounds of overseas buyers. They are the exception which proves the rule. Most of them simply do not have enough confidence in themselves or any of their staff to have sufficient local market knowledge to justify an extended tour of the overseas market.

An even greater source of anxiety is the construction of a permanent overseas base. The pressure to launch such an operation is undoubtedly greater if the product itself carries a heavy servicing burden. When this is the case, a local manager might be installed, in the first instance, as a permanent contact with distributors. Later, perhaps, a permanent branch might be established. This is the point where costs really do begin to mount. Whether they are bearable or not is a question which must ultimately be decided on the basis of market potential, which brings us back again to the very point with which we started, the necessity for a long-term marketing plan.

Transportation

Once you have chosen your selling points and the orders begin to come in, the next question you need to confront is how to ship the goods to the customer in the most direct and cost-effective way. Which way you choose will be determined by:

Speed. In a market with a fast turnover, speed of delivery is essential.

Cost. As a small first-time exporter, cost will be a big factor.

Nature of the Goods. If the goods are fragile or perishable, for example, you will need to consider carefully any long-distance transportation.

Weight and measurement. How bulky are your goods? Volume and size are important determinants in your choice of transportation.

Means of transport / Type of goods	AIR Needs less packing than sea despatch. Speedy	SEA Needs more packing than air despatch. Speed of ship and ports of call vary between lines.	ROAD/SEA Consider packing; lorry weights; drivers' hours; weekend driving restrictions
Low value	–	✓	✓
High value	✓	–	–
Large	✓	✓	✓
Small	✓	–	–
Long-distance fruit, flowers and vegetables	✓	–	–
Hazardous restricted movement	Probably cargo flights only	Possibly freight only ships Surcharges on ferries	✓

Other considerations to be borne in mind for each consignment include:

- Location of consignor and consignee in relation to transport infrastructure
- Transit time
- Frequency of service
- Reliability of service
- Terms of delivery
- Payment terms
- Effect on cash flow of quick/slow delivery

Figure 8.1 *Quick reference table for non-parcel despatches*
Source: *Distribution for the Small Business* by Nicholas Mohr, Kogan Page, 1990.

Packaging. Packaging for overseas has its own problems. You might do well to consult an export packing company.

Weighing carefully each of these factors, you have a choice between four routes to the market overseas: sea, air, road and rail. Figure 8.1 provides a quick reference table for non-parcel despatches.

Despatch routes

Sea

With their bulk loads and increasingly large-scale containerisation, ships provide the cheapest method of transport but one which travels slowly. Certainly, containerisation has produced economies of scale and in recent years the increase in roll-on/roll-off ferries has allowed road or rail transport to be linked with sea transport in a single, combined operation. Exporters no longer have to transport their cargo to a port for loading. Container lines now frequently provide containers on the premises of exporters to provide *full container loads* (FCLs). If you are dealing only in small consignments and always have less than a full container load for shipment, you can deliver your goods to a *container freight station* or *inland clearance depot* to be containerised with others heading for the same destination.

Cargo rates are based on weight or measurement, whichever is the higher. If heavy material is being shipped, payment will be by weight; the goods should display the order number, the destination, the name or mark of the consignee, and the number of separate items in the load.

Air

Although only about a third of world trade goes by air, it is growing in popularity as a means of carriage for the more valuable, urgently required or perishable goods. Nevertheless, its higher costs often seem prohibitive to the small firm except in cases of emergency where the cost factor is outweighed by greater speed and safety. Air freight costs are largely determined by the International Air Transport Association.

If you decide to book space for air cargo, you will find that it follows much the same pattern as booking for a passenger. Each part of the consignment must carry the address of the consignee in line with the information on the way-bill.

A lot of airlines now run a parcels service with overnight delivery. In fact, for small consignments, mail is one of the most convenient forms of transportation; it also involves little documentation. Most air cargo, you should know, is charged by weight rather than volume.

Road

Road is cheaper than air and, given the increasing congestion in the airways, not that much slower. In addition, it offers the added bonus of a door-to-door service.

Road transport across Europe has been increasingly streamlined in recent years through, for example, the development of compatibilities between trailers and towing vehicles, which has enabled a switch-over system to operate at Channel ports.

The same equation of weight with volume is used to determine the cost of your consignments as in sea transport.

Rail

Rail is faster than road over longer distances and, although more vulnerable to industrial action, is usually less subject to long delays than carriage by road.

An express parcels service to Europe run by British Rail includes in its price the costs of customs, handling and documentation. The same equation of weight with volume operates as in the case of sea and road transport.

Documentation

Whichever of these forms you choose, you will need to assemble the following information:

- the name, mark or address of the consignee
- the goods in the consignment
- the mode of transport
- the route chosen
- the number of separate packages
- their weight in metric tonnes and kilograms
- their measurement in cubic metres and centimetres
- their ultimate destination.

Without this information on file, you will be unable to complete the necessary documentation.

The amount of documentation needed has declined in recent years but it is still large enough to be an irritant to the small supplier. If you do not want to set up an export administration department with a member of your clerical staff trained in documentation, you can contact a *freight forwarder*.

Freight forwarding
A freight forwarder will arrange:

- transport and shipping space
- insurance
- documentation
- customs clearance.

Generally, freight forwarders are experienced in transportation and export procedures to particular countries. They can advise on packing, marking and labelling to comply with the requirements of carriers and overseas authorities, and find the most suitable mode of transport.

Many freight forwarders themselves undertake the carriage of goods through their own road services to Europe. Some have entered into containerisation while others have created low-cost systems of consolidated shipments; for example, many offer a 'groupage service' where small consignments may be grouped with those of other exporters, usually resulting in lower freight and other charges.

Express distribution
One of the fastest growing areas of the forwarding business is what is known as *express distribution*. This can be defined as 'the rapid movement of goods on a door-to-door basis providing delivery within a specified time frame'. The advantages of express distribution are:

- *Speed of transit.* This is particularly important if your goods are subject to a short life span or are urgently required by your customers.
- *Published delivery schedules.* These guarantee your buyer delivery at a specified time. If, for example, you are a manufacturer of automotive parts, your customers will require scheduled services which deliver on time.
- *Flexible delivery times.* Large express companies now offer a menu of different types of schedule – same day delivery, next morning and so on – which increases the flexibility of your response to customer demand.
- *Simplified administration.* A large express company should have a streamlined documentation service, perhaps incorporating much of the data required into a single consignment note.

You need to think of transport not as a separate element in its own right but as an integral part of your distributive strategy. Seen in this light, the advantages of express delivery are easily apparent in helping you to hold your customers and beat off the competition of local suppliers.

You need to think of transport as an integral part of your distribution strategy.

Choosing a forwarding agent
The importance of a rapid, scheduled delivery service means that you must take great care in selecting your forwarding agent. Before committing yourself, you need to consider the following points.

First, how many forwarders do you intend to use? One or several? There is a good case for arguing that it is a matter of 'horses for courses'. Some companies are good at handling certain types of goods, while others have specialised over time in dealing with certain countries or along particular routes. If you have a range of products and a multi-market strategy, you would do well to choose an array of companies for the different objectives you have in mind. Counterbalancing this strategy, however, is the old argument that by using an assortment of this kind you will fail to develop the kind of rapport which enables a single operator to understand your company's special needs. If you split your business between too many freight forwarders, there may be insufficient business for each to motivate them to give you the best possible service.

Choose your forwarding agent with care.

What kind of track record has the operator got? Credentials are not easy to examine but at least you can ascertain whether or not operators have a good record for your type of product and market. Find out their major customers and then check with them to see if they are satisfied with their service.

Does the operator have a closed or open distribution system? In other words, does he have a closed system with his own foreign depots, facilities and customs-clearance procedures or is he forced to contract out any of these services at any point? If you yourself were asked at this point to visualise the distribution set-up of the average, fairly large express distributor, you would probably think of it as operating in a sequence running something like this:

(a) Sender;
(b) Collection service;
(c) UK depot;
(d) Air/sea transit;
(e) Central distribution HQ abroad;

(f) Local or regional depot;
(g) Delivery service;
(h) Receiver.

Unfortunately, in many cases your conception would be quite mistaken. Even quite large companies may contract out the service from (d) to (e), losing immediate contact with the goods at that point. Inevitably, you too would also begin to lose touch with your goods at that point.

Imagine you are selling spare parts for machinery to northern Italy. You contact a UK forwarder with a glossy brochure and much talk of a world-wide service, making the typical mistake of the first-time exporter of assuming that the forwarder therefore has a physical presence in the markets to which he guarantees delivery. Granted, your parts are collected on time and shipped accordingly but, unknown to you, your forwarder contracts out the entire operation in Paris to a foreign operator who, in turn, gives way to yet another forwarder in Nice. Unfortunately, the Nice forwarder is temporarily embarrassed by a strike of his drivers. An angry phone call from Turin demands the whereabouts of the parts. Your UK operator cannot help and you are left at the mercy of – to paraphrase Neville Chamberlain – people far away of whom you know nothing.

You must also examine not only the extent of a country's operation but also the width of its scope. This is particularly true if you intend to contract out a great deal of the exporting enterprise along the lines suggested. Already in the USA, for example, large transport companies often provide a marketing service, and this could well be the pattern of the future. In fact, it is already in evidence around our own Channel ports, where companies are beginning to coalesce to offer not only the traditional warehousing and transport facilities but increasingly whole-saling, administrative and even marketing services. They are no longer in the business of simply forwarding freight.

Finally, you will want to know the level of the company's information technology. As a rule, the larger companies will have access to the kind of technology which enables them to key into databases which provide you with the most up-to-date information on routes and services.

This entire sector of your distribution strategy will need to take account of the rapid changes which will affect the whole of European transport in the 1990s. Until recently, few truckers will have escaped unscathed from the catalogue of border barriers which existed before the movement towards the internal market:

- controls caused by varying VAT and excise rates
- adjustments to farm product prices
- veterinary checks enforcing different national health standards
- transport controls, eg licences, national safety regulations
- statistical formalities
- quantity restrictions, eg bilateral trade quotas.

It is true that the costs of these restrictions weighed most heavily with the smaller companies with small consignments and without economies of scale.

In the Europe of the mid-1990s, the position will be very different. To begin with, increasing competition should make transport more efficient. This is one area where we have little to learn from our continental neighbours, having deregulated our transport system almost a generation ago, and the benefits to us should be correspondingly greater. Second only, perhaps, in efficiency to the Dutch, we have a stable and competitive market of about 130,000 hauliers, a figure which has not changed much in recent years. Obviously, our peripheral geographical position means that we will probably never get goods to Spain or Italy as cheaply as the French or Germans, but this is one area at least where we are out at the head of the field in general efficiency. Not only will the system be more efficient, it should be proportionately cheaper to use. Finally, it will almost certainly be faster as competition thins out the field and leaves only the slimmer, leaner runners in the race.

You may, of course, already have experience of transporting goods yourself in the home market and feel you could do the work of carriage more cost effectively yourself using your own transport personnel. If that is the case, you will need to look carefully at what your new market offers in the way of:

- routes, destinations and services
- warehouse locations
- systems of transportation.

Remember that not all markets are as internally accessible as our own. A whole new set of equations is required in terms of cost, distance and reliability. Not surprisingly perhaps, in face of the complexity, many small exporters lose their early determination to go it alone and finally decide to contract out.

Distribution abroad requires a whole new set of equations.

◀ CHAPTER 9 ▶

EXPORT ADMINISTRATION

One of the anxieties which confronts the small or medium-sized exporter who decides to 'go it alone' is how to handle the cluster of activities which we earlier described as forming what is known as export administration. The decisions they involve fall into three main areas:

- quotation
- payment
- documentation.

Quotation

In export administration, the export contract is really the axis upon which all else turns. At a minimum it should:

- describe the goods
- state their price
- describe the method of despatch
- stipulate the mode of payment
- establish guarantees
- list the documents required by the buyers.

In addition to these conditions of sale, it should allocate ownership and responsibility for carriage and insurance at different points of transit, among which the most critical are:

- transportation to docks or airport
- awaiting shipment or loading

- off-loading and storage
- transportation to buyer
- delay.

It is the last of the contractual requirements, the allocation of ownership and responsibility at different points of transit, which, with the price, forms the central element of *the shipping instruction*, which carries a quotation in one of *the international terms of delivery* ('Incoterms'), codified by the International Chamber of Commerce. Each delivery term connects the price to a specific allocation of responsibility between buyer and seller at one of a series of points of transit.

The international terms of delivery connect the price to a specific allocation of responsibility between buyer and seller at the different points of transit.

The choice you face here is a critical one. It is a question of balancing the liabilities you are prepared to incur against the needs of your marketing strategy. The more you protect yourself at the expense of your customer, the less likely you are to repeat the transaction. When you quote, in effect you are making a choice between your own security and the risks of possible future expansion. Quotation and, indeed, the whole armoury of export administration should not be seen as a mere bureaucratic attachment to the rest of the enterprise. It should be selected as an integral part of your marketing strategy. The significance is clear in what is still a common term of delivery.

Terms of delivery

EXW
'Exworks' is the price of the goods collected by the buyer from your factory or warehouse; thus, it is free of delivery charges. The advantage to you of this arrangement is the freedom it brings: not only freedom from responsibility for the goods in transit but also the financial and administrative freedom from having to arrange their shipping and insurance. But at what cost to the customer, who then has to arrange his own freight forwarding, and, ignorant of conditions in the UK, often chooses an operator without depot facilities? The end result of this odyssey is frequently a delayed shipment of damaged goods at costs which had not been originally foreseen.

All in all, the dire effects of quoting 'exworks' cannot be stressed enough. If you do it on a regular basis you will get virtually no repeat business. Your reputation will further suffer if anything goes wrong in transit. Such a quotation is not recommended for anyone wanting to establish a presence in an overseas market.

FAS

'Free alongside ship' is the price of the goods packed ready for shipment and delivered to the quayside of a specified port at your expense. It represents some extension of your liability and cost beyond EXW but still leaves your consignee with the job of getting the goods from the quayside to the vessel. If you are still determined to keep costs down, you can select a named port as near as possible to your premises. Remember, though, that the ports nearest to you may not offer a service to the required port of destination. This is a point which you need to check.

FOB

'Free on board' is, as the name implies, a term originally only used for consignments sent by sea but which was later generalised, somewhat incorrectly, to cover other types of transport. It refers to the price of goods delivered on board at a named port at your expense. Your price, therefore, will need to embrace the freight, documentary and loading charges up to that point. FOB represents a further extension of your liability as an exporter to the actual point of loading, although you still retain the cost benefit of not having to finance freight and insurance beyond that point. These burdens still pass to your customer. Think of the consequences for your marketing strategy, especially if your local competitors make no such imposition on the cost to the customer.

A recent survey found that a significant number of UK exporters are still quoting not only FOB but also exclusively in sterling, a factor which must surely blunt their competitive edge. Physically, indeed, at least in Europe, the whole system of FOB is increasingly out of alignment with developments in transportation. Today's cross-channel ferries carry truckers with door-to-door, all-in prices for consignments which are quickly funnelled through the channel ports. Gone are the days of waiting by the quayside for the coming of the big ships. Yet the costs to the customer still remain.

FRC

'Free carrier' is the term which ought to replace FOB for goods moving by road. The logic is the same except that this time the exporter agrees to deliver the consignment to a land depot named by the buyer. The hand-over generally takes place at the depot of a forwarder who operates a frequent run to the country of destination. If you choose this method, you will carry the costs of delivery to the depot but not beyond.

CIF

'Cost, insurance and freight' represents yet a further extension of your liability, but this time for freight and insurance to the port of destination; consequently, your invoice will cover the costs of these services. The benefit of CIF to you, the exporter, lies in the power it gives you to select the shipping and insurance arrangements at your own rather than the buyer's discretion. As a counterweight to this, you need to consider the drain of these extra costs on your working capital and the extra pressure on your administration of negotiating freight and insurance.

CFR

'Cost and freight' includes freight charges to the port of destination but excludes the cost of insurance.

DCP

'Freight carriage paid' is really a road transport term which allocates to you the responsibility for the goods to a predetermined point, eg DCP Madrid. The advantage to you, the exporter, is that you can choose the carrier and thus control the passage of the goods for a major part of the journey. The service you offer falls short of door-to-door service, as the buyer usually has to arrange for delivery to his own warehouse from the depot. He also has to pay any duty and VAT, to which must be added the costs of local carriage from the depot, which, given the much vaster distances in many larger foreign countries, can seem unreasonably high.

CIP

'Freight carriage and insurance paid' is similar to DCP except that you, as the seller, carry the liability of insurance. Unlike CIF, the insurance cover must be adequate. You will also need to inform your consignee of the details of the cover you have chosen.

DDP

'Delivered duty paid' constitutes the ultimate extension of your responsibility as the supplier. In this quotation, you bear all costs from your premises to those of your customer.

At this end of the scale, the balance of advantages is clear. Agreed, you have total liability but you also have complete control over transit. What is more, your customers know, in a sense, what they are getting for the price they have paid. You could, of course, reduce your costs by excluding such things as customs clearance from the quotation. This may make good sense in the short term, but in the long term it could lessen your powers of penetration. If you have the interests of your customers at heart, this method of quotation is the only way to provide them with a consistent level of service. Put yourself in their shoes. If you had a choice, would you not prefer a door-to-door service of goods from an all-inclusive price list rather than the endless confusion which often attends the other quotations? Not surprisingly, DDP is now the most common type of quotation in Europe.

The terms of delivery should specify the place at which liability is handed over, eg FOB Hull, CIF Cadiz. Quotation will necessarily be in a particular currency. Sterling is easier for the exporter but most importers expect the quotation to be in their own currency. It will greatly annoy a West German buyer, for example, if you quote him in anything other than Deutschmarks.

Most quotations include details of the weight, measurement and packaging of the goods with projected freight and insurance charges. Cargo is normally judged by weight or measurement with the supplier being charged by the tonne or the cubic metre.

If, as a small exporter, you lack the necessary clerical resources to process the documentation, this stage of the operation may seem rather daunting. But do not despair, as both the invoicing and the shipping instruction can be contracted out to a company specialising in export administration.

Payment

Quotation by its very nature anticipates payment at some stage and a number of methods of payment operate in international markets with which you will need to become familiar.

Payment in advance

Payment in advance against an invoice is, if you can get it, by far the best method of payment for you, the exporter. This is because the buyer is effectively extending credit to you; the opposite procedure is the normal method of trade. The inevitable risks to the buyer often lead, therefore, to the demand for some sort of guarantee. The obvious imbalance in risks to the parties concerned inevitably ensures that few export accounts are settled in this way.

Open account

Open account allows all documents to go to the importer; he is allowed to take delivery of the goods and is trusted to pay on the date specified in the conditions of sale. This method of payment is, like payment in advance, at the high-risk end of the scale but with the difference that this time the risks accrue not to the buyer but to you. It may surprise you to know that as a method of payment it is increasingly popular within the European Community. The reason is not hard to fathom. Open accounting is simpler than some other safer methods and its risks diminish with the growth in mutual trust in business integrity which comes from sustained trading over time.

A variation of open accounting is what we call the *consignment account*: an exporter supplies an overseas buyer, often an agent or distributor, to help him to keep stocks at a level sufficient to cover demand over a length of time. The exporter retains ownership of the goods for the duration in question, or at least until the goods are resold, after which period the price is remitted by the buyer.

Open account payment is a risky business. If you are thinking of trading outside certain clearly delimited areas of financial stability in world markets – in other words, anywhere outside western Europe, North America and the Pacific rim – you would do well to consult more seasoned exporters before committing yourself to a method of payment so dependent on trust, stability and commercial goodwill. You will almost certainly find compatriots who have already had their fingers burnt.

Payment against documentary letters of credit

Payment against documentary letters of credit is probably the best method of payment in international trade because it is considered the safest for all concerned. The buyer instructs his bank overseas to authorise a bank in the UK to pay you a specified amount of money within a specific time provided you, in turn, present the bank with documents conforming to the specifications in the documentary letter of credit.

The process by which the documents are transmitted is quite complex, as can be seen from Figure 9.1, but the logic of it is quite

Payment against documentary letters of credit is considered the safest method of payment.

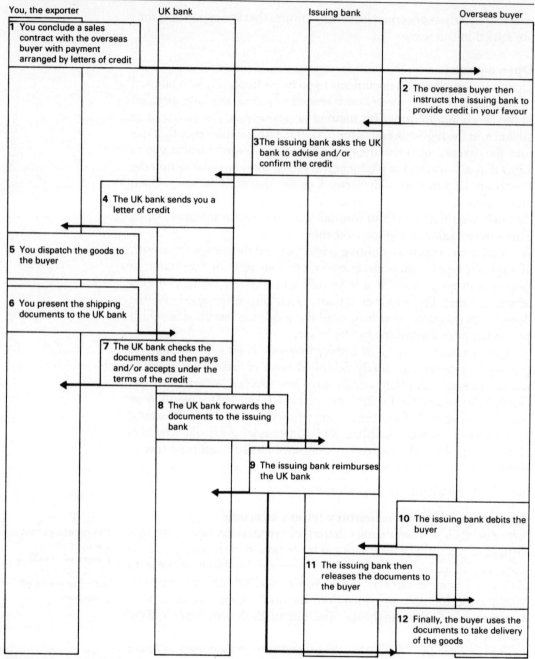

Figure 9.1 *The life cycle of a documentary letter of credit*

simple: the buyer provides the guarantee of payment in return for an assurance from a bank of the delivery to it of the requisite documentation. The letter of credit itself can be opened in either sterling or a foreign currency, depending on the currency of the invoice. As mentioned earlier, many foreign buyers now prefer to be invoiced in their own currency. If invoicing in a foreign currency, you will need to protect yourself against loss through fluctuations in foreign exchange rates during the period of the transaction. Your bank will advise you on how best to proceed.

The most commonly used letters of credit nowadays are *irrevocable*. This means that their terms cannot be altered or revoked without the agreement of the parties concerned. The role of the UK bank in this process is to advise the letters of credit but not necessarily to confirm them. If unconfirmed, the letters carry no undertaking to pay you from the advising bank. They will, therefore, be subject to the issuing bank's capacity to provide the required foreign exchange at the time of presentation.

You will no doubt have sensed the danger here. The promised liquidity may vanish overnight from the banking system of an unstable economy. This is particularly true of banking systems in certain parts of Africa and Latin America. However, a confirmation from the advising bank guarantees payment whatever happens to the issuing bank as long as the conditions of the letters of credit are met. Only such a confirmation can really provide security of payment *without recourse*; that is, without further call upon you, the exporter. The letter of credit is a mandate to pay. In fulfilling this mandate, the bank has no discretion. If the documents presented to it contain errors or inconsistencies, it cannot pay. Nor does its writ extend to the terms of trade. It is up to you to negotiate credit terms that you can comply with. Figure 9.2 shows how the terms are set out in a typical Irrevocable Letter of Credit. You will find that most credits are similar in appearance and contain the following information:

- the type of credit: revocable or irrevocable
- the name and address of the exporter, known as 'the beneficiary'
- the name and address of the importer, known as 'the accreditor'
- the amount of the credit in sterling or a foreign currency
- the name of the party on whom the bills of exchange are to be drawn
- the terms of contract and shipment
- instructions as to the documents against which payment is to be made

The Europa Bank plc

9 Olympia Square, London EC2Y 3NP

Documentary credits department
Date: 26 July 1990
(1) **Irrevocable Credit No**: GMY/14/44
To be quoted on all drafts and correspondence

1. **Beneficiary(ies)** (2)
   Minerva Tools Ltd
   133 Adderley Road
   Rugby E7 1XJ

Advised through:

Accreditor (3)
   The Apollo Co
   Main Street
   Singapore

To be completed only if applicable

Our cable of:

Advised through: refers

Dear Sir(s)

In accordance with instructions received from The Central Bank, we hereby issue in your favour a Documentary Credit for £4408 (say) Four thousand four hundred and eight pounds sterling (4) available by your drafts drawn on us at sight for the 100% CIP (6) invoice value, accompanied by the following documents:

(7)
1. Signed invoice in triplicate.
2. Full set of clean Combined Transport Bills of Lading made out to order and blank endorsed, marked 'Freight paid' and 'Notify The Apollo Co, Main Street, Singapore'.
3. Insurance Policy or Certificate in duplicate, covering Marine and War Risks up to buyer's warehouse, for invoice value of the goods plus 10%

Covering the following goods:
(8) 300 electric saws

(9) To be shipped from London to Singapore CIP (6) not later than 11 August 1990.
(10) Partshipment not permitted Transhipment permitted.

This credit is available for presentation to us until 1 September 1990. (11) Documents to be presented within 21 days of shipment but within credit validity

Drafts drawn hereunder must be marked 'Drawn under The Europa Bank plc, 9 Olympia Square, London EC2Y 3NP'. London branch. Credit number GMY/14/44.

(12) We undertake that drafts and documents drawn under and in strict conformity with the terms of this credit will be honoured upon presentation.

Yours faithfully

Co-signed (Signature No.) Signed (Signature No.)

Figure 9.2 *A documentary letter of credit*

- a description of the goods covered
- the details of shipment: the latest date for shipment and the names of the ports of shipment and discharge.

In this area, above all, accuracy is essential. To avoid mistakes on receipt of the letter, read it with the following checklist of questions in mind:

- Is the credit irrevocable?
- Has it got the confirmation of the advising bank?
- Does it state on the document that it is subject to uniform customs and practice for documentary letters of credit?
- Does it provide for final settlement in the UK?
- Does it contain any spelling errors or verbal ambiguities?
- Do the terms of the credit accord with the terms of the contract of sale? For example, does it correctly describe the nature of the goods? Are the terms of quotation as agreed? Are the details of transportation correctly stated? Are part shipments and trans-shipments allowed? Does it call for the correct transport documents for the carriage employed and can these be obtained exactly as stipulated?
- Does it require any special declarations or certification of documents?
- Does it specify what insurance risks are covered and whether a policy or a certificate is required?
- Can you comply with the terms of the credit? Does the expiry date allow you sufficient time to ship the goods and get the necessary documents presented in time?

If in the light of these questions any amendments are necessary, you should contact your buyer immediately. Having checked the letter of credit thoroughly you will need to prepare the necessary documents. The documents involved are usually:

- an invoice
- a bill of lading
- an insurance certificate/policy
- a bill of exchange.

In preparing them you need to ask yourself the following questions:

- Have you all the required documents?
- Do their details comply with the requirements of the letter of credit? Are they addressed correctly? Does the description of the goods agree with that of the credit? Do the documents showing how the goods were despatched conform to the specifications of the letter of credit? Have the goods been despatched within the time specification of the credit? If the quotation given is C&F, CIF or FOB, or if an 'on-board' document is called for, have you documents that authenticate the loading? Does the insurance cover the risks specified in the credit? Is a policy called for? If so, a certificate is not acceptable. Is certification or legalisation of any document required? If so, this must be effected. Is the bill of exchange correctly drawn and in the appropriate currency?
- Is documentary evidence required for any of the credit terms which do not specifically call for a document, eg copies of cables?
- Are you presenting the documents within the time limits of the credit?

If you feel you need any more help with the processing of letters of credit, you can get a brochure entitled *Uniform Customs and Practice for Documentary Credits* from the International Chamber of Commerce. This brochure sets out the conditions under which banks are prepared to issue and act on commercial credits.

Bills of exchange

We have already seen how bills of exchange figure in the processing of documentary letters of credit but they also form, with the accompanying documentation, a somewhat less secure method of payment in their own right. Put simply, a bill of exchange is a demand for payment of a specified sum at a specified date. It is normally sent with the bill of lading and other documents to a bank overseas, from which the buyer can obtain the documents granting title to the goods by signing the bill of exchange and thereby binding himself to pay the specified sum on the specified date. A bill of acceptance binds the party upon whom it is drawn to accept responsibility for payment.

Bills of exchange are drafted in two forms: *sight drafts*, payable 'at sight' (ie 'on demand'); and *term drafts*, payable 'at a fixed or determinable future time'. Term drafts effectively extend a period of credit to the buyer, known as the *tenor* of the bill. Although not as secure as the use of a letter of credit, the use of a bill of exchange with the shipping documents does enable you to keep some control of your goods because, until the bill is paid or accepted by the buyer, the bank will not release the documents. Consequently, the buyer is unable to take delivery of the goods.

Bills of exchange are sometimes presented unsupported by documentation. This procedure, known as *clean bill collection*, has become increasingly popular in Europe in recent years.

For all methods of payment using a bill of exchange, an alternative exists in the form of a *promissory note*. Such a note is issued by a buyer who promises to pay an exporter a certain sum of money within a specified time.

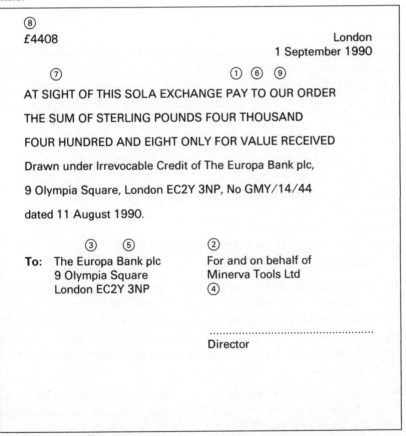

Figure 9.3 *A bill of exchange*

Bills of exchange look rather like cheques. The forms for them may be purchased from a stationer. You can also draw them up on your own company letterhead if you prefer. The example in Figure 9.3 is a sight bill calling for immediate payment by the drawee.

Shipping Documentation

As you will already have gathered, payment in export transactions is determined by the way in which the goods are despatched and the shipping documents are transferred between the principals of the transaction. Let us now look more closely at the different types of accompanying document which serve as a basis for the payment of goods.

Invoice

An invoice is the main document specifying the nature and price of the goods exported.

An invoice is the main document specifying the nature and price of the goods exported. It is the one element of documentation which cannot be contracted out. It will need to meet the requirements of both the exporting and importing country but usually will incorporate the following:

- a record of the goods shipped
- the terms of quotation
- the price of the goods
- the shipping and packaging marks of the bill of lading
- the mode of despatch
- freight and insurance costs
- details of import licences and exchange permits
- weights and measurements.

In the export trade, invoices are not just significant in terms of payment. They operate as a record of the goods shipped and the terms on which they are shipped. In addition, they are critical to the valuation of the goods for tax and duty. It is sometimes necessary to establish that the terms of the contract have been fulfilled and specified for the country of origin through:

- *Certificates of Origin*, which are required by some countries for all goods, and by others for particular items. The necessary documents can be obtained from UK Chambers of Commerce.
- *Certificates of Value and Origin*, which are required by a number of

countries for the invoice of goods for which preferential rates of duty apply. Other countries require certification, counter-signature or authentication by chambers of commerce, consulates or embassies. You will find a number of variations operating and will need to provide for the inevitable costs incurred. Combined certificates of value and origin are obtainable from Croner Publications Ltd and your local Chamber of Commerce.

The Single Administrative Document
Accurate description of goods in invoicing is one of the axes upon which the whole success of the enterprise turns. Clearly, the more standardised and understandable the description the better for all concerned. Standardisation, as we saw earlier in reviewing the European internal market, has been gathering apace in recent years and has considerably reduced the amount of commercial documentation carried en route. One facet of this general movement has been the emergence of the *Single Administrative Document* (SAD) for import and export declarations and transit to and through EFTA (European Free Trade Association) and EC countries.

The SAD carries a *commodity code* to identify the goods, based on an internationally agreed system of classification, the *Harmonised Commodity Description and Coding System* of the Customs Co-operation Council. Within this system, a product receives a unique identification in a numerical code. Unfortunately, these developments do not exhaust the complexity of international product classification. If you want further advice, contact HM Customs and Excise Headquarters, Kings Beam House, Mark Lane, London EC3R 1HE. Details of the 13 classification guides are available in the leaflet (no CDC 100) *Classifying your Imports or Exports*.

There are other methods of making your export declarations which reduce the complexity even further. The *simplified clearance procedure* (SCP) allows approved exporters to clear their goods for export with the SAD or other commercial documents with only skeletal details. The information has to be declared within a specified period after the goods have been shipped. The process has to be authorised by Customs and Excise. You can apply to your local customs office for registration under the scheme.

Bill of lading

In addition to the invoice, a number of documents provide proof that the

A bill of lading is both a contract of carriage and a document of title to the goods.

merchandise has been despatched and loaded. The traditional maritime bill of lading is a receipt for the goods and evidence of the contract between the shipper, normally the exporter, and the shipping company for the carriage and delivery of the goods to the order of the shipper to a named port of destination. The bill is both a contract of carriage and a document of title to the goods. The bill is drawn up either by you, the exporter, or by a freight forwarder. It normally includes:

- a description of the goods
- the terms of carriage
- a named vessel
- a named port.

If the condition of the goods is infringed in any way in transit to the docks, the shipping company may refuse to issue a 'clean' bill of lading. Instead, the bill of lading is 'claused'; that is, given an additional clause pointing to the defect in the goods, which, of course, affects the processing of a documentary letter of credit.

The development of modern transportation has meant that the traditional bill of carriage between two named ports has been increasingly superseded by:

- A *combined transport bill of lading*, which requires neither ports of loading nor destination to be named by the shipper. Instead, it covers transport on a 'door-to-door' or 'depot-to-depot' basis. In other words, it provides comprehensive carriage of the goods from start to finish.
- A *waybill* can replace a bill of lading where no document of title is required for the export transaction. It is often used in open account sales or where trust is not dependent on documentary evidence; for example, in the increasing flow of trade between the different branches of multi-national companies. A way-bill is a receipt for the goods and evidence of their despatch, but it is not a document of title to them.
- An *air waybill* replaces the bill of lading for air freight and has a similar status in commercial law in that it too is non-negotiable.
- A *railway consignment note* is a receipt for goods transported overseas by rail. Like the other types of waybill, it is not a document of title.

Insurance certificate and/or policy
This completes the documentation normally required. Whatever the

method of payment you opt for in the transaction, you will inevitably run the risks of:

- buyer default
- failure of the buyer to obtain foreign currency
- exchange rate fluctuations to your detriment
- exposure to loss and damage en route
- confiscation, expropriation and embargo.

Prior market research of the business climate and customer status should already have alerted you to any risks you run. To cover yourself against both buyer and country risks, you need to contact the Export Credits Guarantee Department (ECGD). This government department has been offering credit insurance to exporters since 1921 and now covers about a fifth of non-oil visible exports. It provides a variety of policies covering short- or long-term transactions, as well as a wide variety of currency arrangements. You do not need to insure the whole of your export turnover, but clearly the greater the spread of insurable risk the lower your premiums will generally be. You can also obtain a one-off deal.

With the basic policy, the short-term guarantee, you are covered for up to 90 per cent of loss from the insolvency of your buyer or his failure to pay within six months of the date on which payment is due. Where a buyer fails to take possession of goods delivered and legal redress is impracticable, you bear the first 20 per cent of the loss with ECGD covering 90 per cent of what remains. Cover for government restraints on trade or contract are rather more generous at, normally, 95 per cent of the loss.

Cover generally begins from the date of shipment, although you can ask for cover from the date of contract. This is called *pre-credit risk cover*. As a rule, it is difficult to get reasonable cover for periods longer than a year between contract and despatch.

Once you are covered by insurance, a bank may discount bills for cash on which you pay interest until such time as the bill is paid by the overseas buyer and the sum remitted. In effect, the insurance policy acts as a form of additional security for export finance. It enables you to obtain finance at a reasonable rate of interest. The discounting arrangement is termed 'foreign bills negotiated' (FBN).

As we have seen, the cargo insurance you obtain is critical to the allocation of responsibility for your goods at the various points of transit between you and your customer. The terms negotiated are then incorporated into the quotation of the shipping instruction. The certificate and policy documents have been dealt with at this juncture because, of course, they are important shipping documents in their own right. Either one or both may be called for.

Accuracy in documentation

Much has been made of the importance of knowledge and precision in documentation. Admittedly, many of the more exacting procedures involved in the process have been removed by the emergence of more systematic and computerised methods of transmitting trade data. These systems, developed by the Simplification of Trade Procedures Board (SITPRO), include one-typing documentation sets, copier-based techniques and microcomputer software packages, which turn out export invoices and other relevant documentation. Even without such facilities your load can, as we have seen, be considerably lightened by contracting out the more onerous tasks. A forwarding agent or other shipper can relieve you of a lot of the documentation, although the actual details of the consignment remain your responsibility.

Failure to maintain standards of excellence in your documentation will cost you dear.

Yet, given all this, we still cannot overlook the importance of prompt and accurate processing of export documents. Failure to maintain standards of excellence in this field will cost you dear. A recent survey found, for example, that almost half the documents lodged under documentary letters of credit were refused on first presentation because they were inaccurate or incomplete. It may surprise you to know that a considerable number of sets of documents are simply left too long in the out-tray. The documents are presented after the period stipulated in the credit or after the letter of credit itself has expired. Even when the documents called for by a letter of credit arrive on time, they frequently contain discrepancies which could be so easily removed by a little prior checking. The list of discrepancies is long enough to fill a research report but among the most common are:

- insufficient information is contained in the bill of lading
- its details do not conform to the specification of the letter of credit
- a discrepancy exists between the description of the goods on the invoice and that in the credit
- the value of the order exceeds the amount specified in the credit
- there is a discrepancy between the values on the invoice and those on the bill of exchange

- the bill of exchange is drawn on the wrong party
- the insurance document enclosed is not of the type specified in the letter of credit
- the risks covered by the policy are not those stipulated in the credit
- the cover is expressed in a currency other than that designated by the credit
- the cover is not effective from the date of despatch
- the goods are simply under-insured
- numbers, marks, weights and spellings differ between documents
- documents are not correctly endorsed
- there is an omission of witnessing signatures where insufficient of the required documents are enclosed.

Errors of this kind can create considerable delays. Letters of credit are, because of the nature of their processing, particularly vulnerable, but other areas of the export enterprise are equally at risk. Errors in invoicing or supporting documentation can block the clearance of your goods on arrival. Rejection of your document can leave you with goods on your hands a long way from home. You may then need to arrange storage and extended insurance cover. Indeed, you may have little prospect of reselling them without considerable commercial loss. In contrast, successful expedition of these matters facilitates the rapid transit of your goods and is, by that very token, an effective means of export sales promotion.

◀ CONCLUSION ▶

It is not always an easy task to convince the small firm with less than 100 staff and a turnover perhaps of little more than a million to enter the strange and often exotic world of the overseas market. Domestic marketing is simpler and safer. True, a stronger customer base in a narrow but stable niche of the home market is a source of security, but only as long as it lasts. In a global market, no home base is ever completely safe from predators, and these are arriving on our doorsteps in increasing numbers every day, in the shape of the continental Europeans and the Pacific nations. If you are not pulled into overseas adventures you may very soon be pushed.

Whatever the momentum which took you there, you will then find yourself alone with the problems of marketing your product in an entirely new environment. Much of the earlier part of this book was devoted to the theme that marketing in this sense is by no means synonymous with selling and promotion. A good sales drive is critical to the success of the operation but only as the final cutting edge of the weapon of marketing strategy. I have been told on numerous occasions that if you have a good product and sales staff technically conversant with it, you should have no problems selling. But if you, as a marketer, have done your job effectively, the goods should sell very easily. You might say that the ultimate aim of marketing is to render the act of selling superfluous.

The key to marketing success is a recognition of the sovereignty of the consumer. The key to marketing success is a recognition of the sovereignty of the consumer. A product may have much in the abstract to recommend it, but it will get nowhere unless it is packaged, priced and placed in a way which catches the attention of its potential consumers. It may sound heretical but this statement itself is almost a contradiction in terms, for good quality control is itself usually a facet of a general marketing orientation. Thus, it was not the quality of Japanese products alone that

104

wiped out large sections of the British motor cycle and German cutlery industry a generation ago, but that quality was the ultimate concrete manifestation of the Japanese marketing strategy.

With high fixed costs and a home market unable to absorb their excessive investment, Japanese companies have been forced to sell abroad. Once overseas, it has been argued, they simply exploited the marketing sensitivity that they had developed at home. Indeed, it has been said that the same principles apply to exporting as in marketing generally. You must still set marketing objectives, choose your markets, develop marketing positions and mixes, and keep a constant eye on all these processes through marketing control. But you must also bear in mind that the differences between cultures abroad are, as we have seen, phenomenal. There are countries in the world with only the most primitive promotional channels and systems of distribution, without any of the large retail chains to which we are accustomed. At the other extreme are countries with a sophistication in all these matters, far in advance of our own.

In all these countries, the same marketing principles apply, but in a context rendered much more intricate by a geographical and cultural distance which leaves you without any safe, prior assumptions about how your goods are likely to reach your customer and how, at the end of the line, their ultimate consumer is likely to respond to them.

As a first-time exporter, you will enter a new and turbulent environment in which unpredictability is often the rule. The challenge could put your company to its severest test. New objectives may be needed; a new strategy forced upon you. If we lived in a totally rational world, companies would scan their environments for openings, set appropriate objectives and develop strategies. But the real world is nothing like this. As an operator on the home market, you will already have management systems designed with objectives in mind, but these could prove increasingly irrelevant to the requirements of your developing export enterprise. The element of inertia which is always present in management systems will work against you and make it difficult to turn your company around.

If the export drive begins to take off, then, at some stage, you will need to take a fresh look at your own operation. Much was made earlier of the way in which companies are often oriented to a particular focus in finance, production or sales. To turn such a company to a marketing orientation requires not only a change of perspective but also the incorporation of new management systems to support the marketing drive. Radical changes in management structures require a great deal of formal planning. The problem for you as a small-business person is that you have probably been so busy in the early years searching for funds, customers, equipment and materials that you have had little time for formal planning of any description.

All companies start out with four simple functions: raising and managing capital; producing the product or service; selling it; and keeping the books. On my tours around small companies, I have been surprised by how big the operation has to grow before any of these functions are relinquished from the managing director's sphere of responsibility. Relinquish he must, however, or the company will simply not be able to operate effectively beyond a certain point. Additional tasks in market research or promotion are generally passed over to the sales manager, who often gives them little more than a half-hearted commitment. As the company expands, such services are required on a more specialised and continuous basis. At this stage, the sales manager may hire someone to do the marketing for him. Under the sheer pressure of work, the sales department will begin to give shape to a marketing section. Eventually, a marketing department will separate out. The impact of the export drive is to speed up the momentum of this movement towards a marketing culture at certain critical points. Ultimately, therefore, a decision to export on a long-term basis is a commitment, whether conscious or not, to develop the kind of management structures which support such a culture.

If you wish to avoid this commitment while thus maintaining your export drive, one alternative exists, which can remain a half-way house for many years. You can simply contract out the operations in those sectors of your company in which you do not wish, as yet, to encourage any internal organisational growth. You will need to do an audit of the entire operation early on to decide which of its stages you will handle yourself and which you will contract out:

- Will you do your own marketing research or use a consultancy?
- Will you prepare your own advertising or use an agency from start to finish?
- Will you develop your own transport or hire a delivery company?
- Will you use your own sales staff or an agent or importing distributor?
- Will you do your own export administration or contract out as much as you possibly can?

Much was made earlier of the efficiency that these intermediaries develop through long experience and the scale of their operations, but the costs to you are high. The question you must ask is: Are these costs higher than the cost in money, time and psychological stress of setting up the organisational infrastructure to support these functions?

Clearly, this compromise cannot last for ever. Growth inevitably complicates the division of labour to a point at which contracting out on a large scale creates too many problems of control to be viable, which is why, of course, most large companies have their own marketing departments. Coping with such problems pushes your company not only towards a marketing culture but also towards what is known as a 'planning culture'. A company with such a culture has a number of characteristics which are a key to survival in the international market. It encourages its managers to analyse systematically the relationship between strategies and objectives. It extracts what is implicit in their performance criteria and makes it explicit. Finally, in doing all this, it creates a more organic co-ordination of effort and a greater sense of collective mission.

Exporting is, as we have seen, a prime mover in this general process. It encourages innovative thinking and collective planning. You have to work especially hard to win and hold customers in distant markets. It must surely, therefore, sharpen your competitive edge.

You have to work especially hard to win and hold customers in distant markets.

Yet it brings other boons as well. A larger market-place is also a potential source of greater funds for long-term investment and an added protection against the sudden shock of a fall-off of demand on the home market. It is also an intriguing strategic window on the world of international trade, which can reveal quite unexpected possibilities of growth and transformation, the emergence of contracts and tenders, and potential for mergers and for a host of reciprocal or other collaborative ventures with both British and foreign firms. Such apples of the Hesperides are there for the taking, albeit late in the day, and then only to those who have lasted the race.

◀ FURTHER INFORMATION ▶

If you are a first-time exporter, one of the major problems you will face is where to find the information you need. A massive amount of information is available but through networks which in many cases have grown in isolation from one another. As a consequence, I have met quite seasoned exporters who have been completely unaware of whole areas of data relevant to their needs. What is lacking, in fact, is a central communications network to unite the various sources in a single grid. The nearest equivalent is the databases of the Department of Trade and Industry (DTI), although these by no means encompass all of the information available. In the absence of a central network, the database here attempts to list the major sources to tap into at the different stages of the export enterprise. The list is by no means exhaustive, but it should provide enough points of contact to set you on your way.

Exporting in general

If you want some hints on how to begin planning your export drive, *The Export Initiative* of the DTI can give you some sound advice on the whole field of export marketing research and promotion. The DTI also offers a consultancy service under the *marketing initiative*, which is managed on its behalf by the Chartered Institute of Marketing. For information on both these ventures, contact your DTI regional office.

Further information and training is also available from the *Institute of Export*, Export House, 64 Clifton Street, London EC2A 4HB (Tel: 071-247 9812) and the *Chartered Institute of Marketing*, operating under its own aegis.

By the way, do not neglect the *Small Firms Service*, as it is often a useful first point of contact. You can get in touch by dialling 100 and asking for 'freefone enterprise' or by writing to the Small Firms and Tourism Division of the Department of Employment, Steele House, Tothill Street, London SW1H 9NF.

Overseas markets

Once you begin your market research, you will find that there is no shortage of information in print on virtually every market you are likely to target. Indeed, your main problem initially will be how to sift through the mass of statistics to get to the often quite limited information you need on a particular market segment.

The DTI's magazine *Overseas Trade* is published 10 times a year and is available to exporters together with information packs. It has some useful information on world markets and can keep you up to date with recent developments. For a specimen copy, contact your DTI regional office.

Even in this age of high-tech, you might find that the most lucrative source of information is your central reference library. Any large urban reference or business library will hold *Overseas Trade Statistics of the United Kingdom*, a monthly publication by the HMSO which gives a breakdown of UK imports and exports by country of origin and destination. Once you have obtained the classification number for your product, refer to HMSO's annually published *Guide to the Classification of Overseas Trade Statistics*.

Not too far along the shelves you should also come across trade journals and directories, Organisation for Economic Co-operation and Development forecasts, European Commission publications, and World Bank and International Monetary Fund publications.

You will also find compilations of economic data on the European Community in journals such as *European Business*, *European Trends*, *The EC Bulletin* and *Euromonitor*.

Beyond the European markets, *The World of Information* publishes some very useful data on the major trading regions of the world. Not to be overlooked, either, are newspapers which produce country surveys, such as the *Financial Times* and *The Economist*. *The Economist*'s 'intelligence unit' has recent data and commentary on almost every country in the world.

Finally, a number of libraries have their own purpose-built databases painstakingly compiled by librarians from newspaper cuttings and photostats of various sources. I myself recently stumbled upon one such gold-mine, a database on Europe 1992, while researching this very topic. Without exaggeration, it saved me weeks of work.

For those who haven't got the time to browse through a reference library, more easily accessible information on world markets is available from: the *British Overseas Trade Information Service* (BOTIS); a database available at the *Export Market Information Centre*, 1 Victoria Street, London SW1H OET (Tel: 071-215 5444), which provides information on products, markets, overseas agents, distributors and promotional events, as well as an index to other information sources; and the *Export Intelligence Service* (EIS), a computerised system of information on overseas markets. Available to subscribers only, the EIS gathers information from diplomatic service posts and other contact points. It allows access to information received over the previous three years and in a form which matches computer-coded requirements. It covers every country in the world and incorporates over 10,000 products or services. For a free demonstration, contact you DTI regional office.

The information on overseas markets covered so far has been collated under classifications with the general public in mind. Information more tailored to your particular needs can be obtained from the *Export Marketing Research Scheme* (EMRS), which provides free consultation with EMRS advisers and funding for research conducted either in-house or by consultants. For in-house research by your own staff, 50 per cent of the agreed expenditure can be provided up to a maximum of £40,000 per project. In-house funding does not cover EC countries; this restriction does not apply to research undertaken by outside consultants. In addition to field research funding, the EMRS will pay up to one-third of the cost of a maximum of two published research reports in a year, which can focus your own research activity and may be sufficient as a database for a small company on a tight budget. The scheme is run on behalf of the DTI by the Association of British Chambers of Commerce. Details of funding can be obtained from the Association of British Chambers of Commerce, 4 Westwood House, Westwood Business Park, Coventry CV4 8MS (Tel: 0203 694484) or any regional office of the DTI.

At a further stage in your planning, you may also require samples of competing products. These can be obtained from the export service division of the DTI. To find out more about this scheme, contact your DTI regional office.

If you conform to the modal pattern for British exporters, at least one of your targets is likely to be in the European market. If so, you cannot afford to ignore the enormous amount of legislation on physical, technical and fiscal barriers to trade which has been passing down the Community pipeline since the Single European Act of July 1987. So significant has been the work done that it now constitutes a separate field of data with its own distinctive line of commentary and analysis. For the beginner in this field, a good introduction is the *DTI Single Market Action Pack*. For information, ring the 1992 hotline on 081-200 1992.

There are also some useful guides on the state of the game in current legislation, most notably *Deloitte's 1992 Guide*, published by Butterworths (London), and *Croner's Europe*, Croner Publications, Croner House, London Road, Kingston-upon-Thames, Surrey KT2 65R (Tel: 081-547 3333).

If you are interested in the more general economic consequences of the single market for companies, the most comprehensive piece of research, although one whose predictions of benefits probably err on the side of optimism, is *The European Challenge 1992: The Benefits of a Single Market* by Paolo Cecchini, published by Wildwood House, Aldershot, Hants (1988).

So extensive have the tentacles of EC intervention in commerce become that it is not easy to keep abreast of current events, especially in the field of investment and training. A useful channel of information is the Small and Medium-sized Enterprise Task Force, set up by the European Commission as part of its enterprise policy. It provides a useful network of data on EC research and development projects, training and investment, as well as a channel of communication on current legislation to the European Commission itself.

A similar facility is available through *Spearhead*, a new EC single-market database, allowing access to recent EC legislation. It is available through *Profile Information*, which is part of the Financial Times group. Non-members should phone 0932 761444. A £110 subscription entitles a user to key in to the full text of the relevant legislation. It provides details of measures adopted or yet to be implemented and proposals under discussion. A government contact point is given for additional help in understanding directives and how they may affect a particular business. The system responds to a few simple commands, easily managed by those with no previous experience of data searching. A wide range of personal computers is suitable for accessing Spearhead. Many Chambers of Commerce and trade associations have such systems and subscribe to services with access to this data box. It was through this system that one client in the drinks industry discovered that under new European standardisation, not only had he to list contents and additives on the outside of the bottle with special syntax and vocabulary in letters of a particular size, but he was also required to use a special type of glue to keep the label on.

On the subject of technical standards in general, both European and world-wide, the British Standards Institution (BSI), through its technical help to exporters, provides data on: national environmental and safety legislation; technical standards; and certification. It also offers: a technical enquiry service for routine enquiries; a consultancy service; technical research; and a library of over 500,000 standards for 160 countries with English translations. For information, contact Technical Help for Exporters, Linford Wood, Milton Keynes, MK14 6LE (Tel: 0908 220022).

Trade associations are also a useful mine of information on technical standards and are alert to the process of harmonisation in the EC.

If you are involved in a highly innovative field, you will also need to be *au fait* with the patent legislation which affects your product. Patent and industrial property investigations can be undertaken with the help of the DTI's patent office. For information, phone 071-829 6512.

If you are a firm looking to tender abroad, you will need information on openings for supply and subcontracting in overseas markets. Fortunately, in what is often a difficult area to break into, there is plenty of help available from: the DTI Projects and Export Policy Division, 1 Victoria Street, London SW1H OET, whose world aid section offers advance information on the work of multi-lateral development agencies; and the Crown Agents, St Nicholas House, St Nicholas Road, Sutton, Surrey SM1 1EL (Tel: 081-643 3311).

Information on European contracts and tenders, in particular, can be obtained from European Information Centres (EICs). EICs provide data on public procurement contracts and procedures for tendering. To find out more, dial 100 and ask for 'freefone enterprise'.

Finally, if you are thinking of looking for a European partner, get in touch with your DTI regional office or an EIC and find out how to plug into the European Commission's marriage bureau, the *Business Co-operation Network* (BC-Net). You might also try your local Chamber of Commerce. Many chambers circularise their members with lists of foreign firms looking for a British contact.

Promotion

As a first-time exporter, you will confront the novel task of how to organise a promotional campaign to market your product overseas. Fortunately, help can be found from a number of sources.

Publicity

The DTI give advice on publications and provide specialist help from journalists at the Central Office of Information (COI). To find out more, contact your DTI regional office.

Check your local library for the *Advertising Blue Book* for a selection of agencies with overseas connections.

Missions

The DTI can give financial assistance to participation in an outward mission if it is sponsored by an approved trade association or Chamber of Commerce. The sum offered is scarcly a prince's ransom, usually a percentage of the total cost of travel and subsistence, but may be very welcome to a small company operating on a tight, promotional budget. Data on trades and missions can be obtained from DTI Fairs and Promotions Branch, Dean Bradley House, Horseferry Road, London SW1P 2AG (Tel: 071-276 3000).

Local authorities can sometimes provide useful EC contacts with European Chambers of Commerce through their twinning arrangements.

Exhibiting

The DTI can offer financial support and advice in: provision of a basic stand and display aids at reduced rates; translation; shipping; publicity; and agents and distributors. It will even go so far as to contact overseas exhibition organisers and book space for you in the right section of the fair. For more information on the range of assistance it offers, contact DTI Fairs and Promotions Branch or a DTI regional office. A booklet on the pitfalls involved in visiting markets is available in the *Hints to Exporters* series produced by the DTI.

Languages

If you need any help in tooling up your own language skills or in organising a crash course for one of your staff, you can contact the new languages-for-export centres, a network of centres usually based in universities and polytechnics, which cover the whole of the country on a regional basis. Contact your DTI regional office for further information.

Distribution

One of the greatest anxieties of first-time exporters is how to find out what routes are available for getting their goods to the overseas market. Most, as we have seen, operate initially through export houses. For information on the best one to choose for your niche of the market, contact British Export Houses Association, 16 Dartmouth Street, London SW1H 9BL (Tel: 071-222 5419). For a fee, you can insert a notice in the association's *Export Enquiry Circular*.

If still in doubt, you could also contact your local Chamber of Commerce, whose export development adviser should have some knowledge of local export houses in your region.

Agents and distributors can be sought through advertising in the trade and national press; approached in writing following identification in trade directories; or contacted personally at overseas fairs and exhibitions.

The DTI database on business contacts can rapidly produce a short list of names of agents or distributors who are likely to be interested in your product and whom you could approach directly. The DTI can also undertake an investigation through diplomatic service posts of local contacts and their trading interests, scope and capabilities, other principals, warehousing and distribution facilities, sales force and after-sales support.

Additional contacts exist in the shape of the Institute of Export, 64 Clifton Street, London EC2A 4HB (Tel: 071-247 9812), which can offer you some useful advice on both selection and contractual legislation. Similarly well equipped to help are national and local Chambers of Commerce.

Critical to the success of distribution is the timely and economical transport of your goods to the overseas market. Few exporters take this on themselves in their first venture. The best people to contact are freight forwarders. You can either contact the British International Freight Association, Redfern House, Browells Lane, Feltham, Middlesex TW13 7EP (Tel: 081-844 2266); or obtain *The Freight Forwarders Year Book*. There is also a booklet entitled *A Brief Introduction to Freight Forwarding*. You might find it useful to ring round a few in your area and see what kind of service they offer. Freight charges and expenses can vary considerably, so it is worth shopping around.

Export administration

As we have seen, no matter how you decide to export abroad you are going to be involved in at least some administration. The major administrative problem is, of course, export documentation. With respect to documentary letters of credit, a useful list of questions to bear in mind when processing these can be obtained from the Documentary Credits Department Wholesale Operations, Midland Bank plc, 3 Lower Thames Street, London EC3R 6HA (Tel: 071-260 4393; fax: 071-260 4640).

The Simplification of Trade Procedures Board (SITPRO) provides a list of specialists in export documentation. SITPRO can also bypass the paperwork by sending documents by electronic data exchange. This is available to anyone with an ordinary desk-top microcomputer and a telephone connection, or access to a dedicated computer link or network. For further information, contact SITPRO, Almack House, 26–28 King Street, London SW1Y 6QW (Tel: 071-930 0532).

Alternatively, the entire operation – transport, documentation, customs clearance and insurance – can be handled by freight forwarders, a list of which can be obtained from the British International Freight Association, Redfern House, Browells Lane, Feltham, Middlesex TW13 7EP (Tel: 081-844 2266). You could also consult *Croner's Reference Book for Exporters*, which is available on subscription and updated monthly, and the monthly *Export Digest*.

The principal terms of quotations are contained in *Incoterms*, which is obtainable from the International Chamber of Commerce, British National Committee, Centre Point, New Oxford Street, London WC1A 1QB.

Finally, information on how to insure yourself against buyer default and other risks can be obtained from: Association of British Insurers, Aldermary House, 10–15 Queen Street, London EC4N 1TT (Tel: 071-248 4477; fax: 071-489 1120); British Insurance and Investment Brokers Association, 14 Bevis Marks, London EC3A 7NT (Tel: 071-623 9043); Export Credits Guarantee Department (Project Group), PO Box 272, Export House, 50 Ludgate Hill, London EC4M 7AY (Tel: 071-382 7000; telex: 0222 883601; fax: 071-382 7649); or ECGD (Short-term Insurance), New Crown Building, Cathays Park, Cardiff CF1 3NH (Tel: 0222 824000; telex: 0222 497305; fax: 0222 824003).

◀ FURTHER READING ▶

Distribution for the Small Business, Nicholas Mohr, Kogan Page, 1990

Elements of Export Practice, 2nd edition, Alan Branch, Chapman & Hall, 1985

Export for the Small Business, 2nd edition, Henry Deschampsneufs, 1988, revised 1990

Export Trade: Law and Practice of International Trade, Clive M Schmitthoff, Stevens & Sons, 1986

Exporter and Forwarder: The Professional Guide 1990, British International Freight Association, 1990

Exporting, James Dudley, Longmans, 1989

How to Make Exhibitions Work for Your Business, John Talbot, 1989

ICC Guide to Incoterms, International Chamber of Commerce, 1990

Report on the Market for Express Goods Services between the UK and Europe, North America, and the Far East, Institute of Logistics and Distribution Management, 1989

Selling to Europe: A Practical Guide to Doing Business in the Single Market, Roger Bennett, Kogan Page, 1991

Successful Exporting for Small Businesses, David Royce, Letts, 1990

The Transport and Distribution Manager's Guide to 1992, David Lowe, Kogan Page, 1989

Never Take No for An Answer: A Guide to Successful Negotiation, 2nd edition, Samfrits Le Poole, Kogan Page, 1991

◀ INDEX ▶